G000019827

Cycle TOURS

Around Bristol and Bath

Nick Cotton

First published in 2002 by
Philip's, a division of
Octopus Publishing Group Ltd
2-4 Heron Quays
London E14 4JP

First edition 2002
First impression 2002

Based on the original Ordnance Survey Cycle Tours series
first published by Philip's and Ordnance Survey®.

ISBN 0-540-08196-5

The route maps in this book are reproduced from
Ordnance Survey® Landranger® mapping.

Text and compilation copyright © Philip's 2002

Ordnance Survey®

This product includes mapping data licensed from Ordnance
Survey® with the permission of the Controller of Her Majesty's
Stationery Office. © Crown copyright 2002. All rights reserved.
Licence number 100011710

To the best of the Publishers' knowledge, the information in this
book was correct at the time of going to press. No responsibility
can be accepted for any error or their consequences.

The representation in this book of a road, track or path is no
evidence of the existence of a right of way.

Ordnance Survey and the OS Symbol are registered trademarks
of Ordnance Survey, the national mapping agency of Great
Britain.

Printed and bound in Spain by Cayfosa-Quebecor

Photographic acknowledgements

Nick Cotton 55, 61, 107 • Derek Forss 43 • Colin Molyneux
Associates 68, 73 • Pitkin Pictorials Limited 110 • Judy Todd 6,
13, 18, 37, 49, 85, 94, 103

Contents

Abbreviations and symbols

Page diagrams

The page diagrams on the introductory pages show how the map pages have been laid out, how they overlap and if any inset maps have been used.

This section of the route is shown on pages 20 and 21

This overlap area appears at the foot of pages 20 and 21 and at the top of pages 22 and 23

This section of the route is shown on pages 22 and 23

This area is shown as an inset on page 21

20   21

Richmond

22   23

Cross-profiles

The vertical scale is the same on each diagram but the horizontal scale varies according to the length of the route.

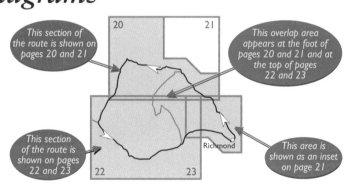

Sychnant Pass

Cefn Coch

Rowen

Start/finish

Start/finish

Legend to 1:50 000 maps

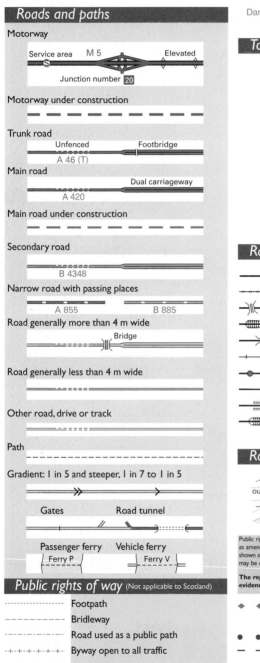

Roads and paths

Motorway

Service area   M 5   Elevated

Junction number **20**

Motorway under construction

Trunk road

Unfenced   Footbridge

A 46 (T)

Main road

Dual carriageway

A 420

Main road under construction

Secondary road

B 4348

Narrow road with passing places

A 855   B 885

Road generally more than 4 m wide

Bridge

Road generally less than 4 m wide

Other road, drive or track

Path

Gradient: 1 in 5 and steeper, 1 in 7 to 1 in 5

Gates   Road tunnel

Passenger ferry   Vehicle ferry

Ferry P   Ferry V

Public rights of way (Not applicable to Scotland)

```
············ Footpath
– – – – – – – Bridleway
–·–·–·–·– Road used as a public path
-+-+-+-+- Byway open to all traffic
```

Danger Area   Firing and test ranges in the area.
Danger! Observe warning notices

Tourist information

🄳	🄸	Information centre, all year / seasonal
🄿		Parking
✕		Picnic site
⸜⸝		Viewpoint
𝝠		Camp site
⚌		Caravan site
▲		Youth hostel
▨		Selected places of tourist interest
☎		Public telephone
☎		Motoring organisation telephone
Γ		Golf course or link
PC		Public convenience (in rural areas)

Railways

▬▬▬	Track: multiple or single
┼┼┼	Track: narrow gauge
)⧖(	Bridges, footpath
⬡····⬡	Tunnel
⌇	Viaduct
┼┼┼	Freight line, siding or tramway
●■○ a b	Station, (a) principal, (b) closed to passengers
╫LC	Level crossing
⫯⫯⫯⫯⫯	Embankment
⬡⬡⬡	Cutting

Rock features

outcrop   650   cliff   –600   scree

Public rights of way indicated by these symbols have been derived from Definitive Maps as amended by the latest enactments or instruments held by Ordnance Survey and are shown subject to the limitations imposed by the scale of mapping. Further information may be obtained from the appropriate County or London Borough Council

The representation of this map of any other road, track or path is no evidence of the existence of a right of way.

◆ ◆ ◆   National Trail, Long Distance Route, selected recreational paths

● ● ●   National/Regional Cycle Network

– – –   Surfaced cycle route

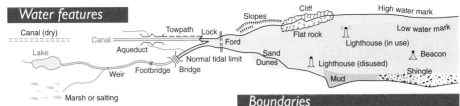

Water features

Canal (dry)
Canal
Lake
Aqueduct
Weir
Footbridge
Marsh or salting

Towpath Lock
Ford
Bridge
Normal tidal limit

Slopes
Cliff
Flat rock
Sand
Dunes
Mud

High water mark
Low water mark
Lighthouse (in use)
Lighthouse (disused)
Beacon
Shingle

General features

⋏——⋏——⋏	Electricity transmission line (with pylons spaced conventionally)
> --> -->	Pipeline (arrow indicates direction of flow)
	Buildings
	Public buildings (selected)
	Bus or coach station
	Coniferous wood
	Non-coniferous wood
	Mixed wood
	Orchard
	Park or ornamental grounds
	Quarry
	Spoil heap, refuse tip or dump
ⵘ	Radio or TV mast
♦	Church or chapel with tower
♦	Church or chapel with spire
+	Church or chapel without tower or spire
○	Chimney or tower
⌀	Glasshouse
⊹	Graticule intersection at 5' intervals
Ⓗ	Heliport
△	Triangulation pillar
ⵊ	Windmill with or without sails
ⵊ	Windpump

Boundaries

+ — + — + National
-o- -o- -o- -o- -o- London borough
National park or forest park
NT National Trust
—·—·—·— County, region or islands area
+ + + + + District

NT open access
NT limited access

Abbreviations

P	Post office
PH	Public house
MS	Milestone
MP	Milepost
CH	Clubhouse
PC	Public convenience (in rural areas)
TH	Town hall, guildhall or equivalent
CG	Coastguard

Antiquities

VILLA	Roman
Castle	Non-Roman
⚔	Battlefield (with date)
☆	Tumulus
+	Position of antiquity which cannot be drawn to scale
𝔐	Ancient monuments and historic buildings in the care of the Secretaries of State for the Environment, for Scotland and for Wales and that are open to the public

Heights

=50= Contours are at 10 metres vertical interval

·144 Heights are to the nearest metre above mean sea level

Heights shown close to a triangulation pillar refer to the station height at ground level and not necessarily to the summit

From Thornbury to Berkeley in the Severn Vale

An exploration of the southern end of the Vale of the Severn. The ride starts from the attractive town of Thornbury and goes as far north as Berkeley, with its famous castle and museums. The route is an essentially flat ride through lush pastures, passing stone-built houses with old red tiles weathered green by age. There are good views across the Severn to the Forest of Dean and Wales at several points, notably at Shepperdine.

 Start

The High St, Thornbury

🅿 Long-term parking at the back of the supermarket (follow signs)

 Distance and grade

52 km (33 miles)
🖊 Easy

 Terrain

Mainly flat or undulating in the Vale of the Severn, with one steep hill from Olveston to Old Down

 Nearest railway

Yate, 8 km (5 miles) from the route at Tytherington, or Severn Beach, 10 km (6 miles) from the route at Olveston. (These stations are not open on Sundays.) Alternatively, Bristol Parkway, 13 km (8 miles) from Tytherington

◄ *Berkeley Castle*

Thornbury   Tytherington   Townwell   Berkeley

Places of interest

Berkeley 15

A quiet Georgian town dominated by the castle, Berkeley also has a fine early English church, which contains many memorials to the Berkeley family. The churchyard contains the grave of Edward Jenner (1749–1823) pioneer of smallpox vaccination who was born here.

Berkeley Castle 15

Situated south of the town to Berkeley, this Norman fortress, built in the reign of Henry II, has been transformed into a magnificent stately home surrounded by terraced Elizabethan gardens. It has been the ancestral home of the Berkeley family for over 800 years. A butterfly farm set in a walled garden houses many species of exotic and British butterflies.

The Kitchen Garden, Old Down House, Tockington 26

Victorian estate with restaurant, country good shop and gift shop. Old Down House is the centre of a mixed dairy and arable farm with the Kitchen Garden Restaurant situated in converted stables.

The Jenner Museum 15

Museum and medical centre established by the Jenner Trust and British Society for Immunology in memory of Edward Jenner, medical scientist and naturalist, who discovered the smallpox vaccine after recognising the link between cowpox and smallpox.

Refreshments

White Hart PH 🍽🍽, **Littleton-upon-Severn**
The Anchor PH 🍽🍽, **Oldbury-on-Severn**
The Swan PH 🍽, **Tytherington**
The Windbound PH 🍽, **Shepperdine**
Plenty of choice in **Berkeley**
Tea and coffee at Old Down Kitchen Garden, **Tockington**

Shepperdine

Oldbury-on-Severn

Littleton-upon-Severn

Olveston

Old Down

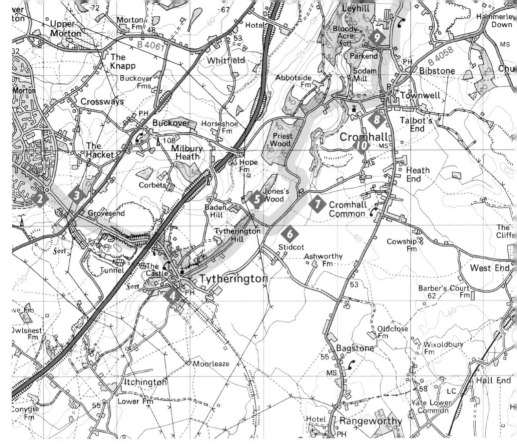

1 From the High Street, follow signs for Gloucester (A38). At roundabout by the Royal George PH turn R past the Plough PH onto Quaker Lane. After 300 m (yd) L by car park onto Gillingstool 'Grovesend, Gloucester'

2 At roundabout SA 'Gloucester, Bristol (A38)'

3 At T-j with A38, L then 1st R 'Quarry ½, Tytherington'

4 Opposite The Swan PH in Tytherington L onto Baden Hill Road (NS)

5 At T-j R (NS)

6 At next T-j L 'Cromhall'

7 **Easy to miss**. After 800 m (½ mile) 1st L

8 At X-roads with B4058 L then L again 'Parkend'

9 At T-j R (NS). At next T-j L (NS)

➡ *next page*

22 2½ km (1½ miles) after Oldbury on sharp LH bend by triangle of grass (Thornbury and Kington signposted to the left) turn R

23 Ignore 1st L to Olveston and Elberton. Take 2nd L by triangle of grass (same sign). Go past White Hart PH in Littleton

24 At offset X-roads with B4461 R then L

25 At T-j in Olveston L then L uphill opposite White Hart PH on Vicarage Lane

26 Steep climb. At T-j at top of hill L then L again on Foxholes Lane 'Elberton 1½'. 400 m (yd) on left, Old Down Kitchen Garden Tea Shop and Restaurant – worth a visit!

27 At T-j with busy road (B4461) R for 800 m (½ mile) then 1st L 'Kington, Mumbleys'

28 At T-j R (NS)

29 After 1½ km (1 mile) at next T-j R 'Thornbury Centre'

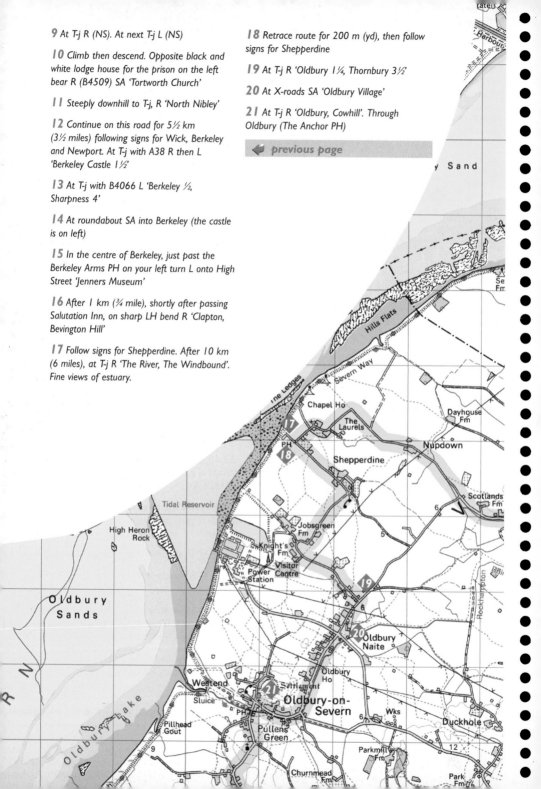

9 At T-j R (NS). At next T-j L (NS)

10 Climb then descend. Opposite black and white lodge house for the prison on the left bear R (B4509) SA 'Tortworth Church'

11 Steeply downhill to T-j, R 'North Nibley'

12 Continue on this road for 5½ km (3½ miles) following signs for Wick, Berkeley and Newport. At T-j with A38 R then L 'Berkeley Castle 1½'

13 At T-j with B4066 L 'Berkeley ½, Sharpness 4'

14 At roundabout SA into Berkeley (the castle is on left)

15 In the centre of Berkeley, just past the Berkeley Arms PH on your left turn L onto High Street 'Jenners Museum'

16 After 1 km (¾ mile), shortly after passing Salutation Inn, on sharp LH bend R 'Clapton, Bevington Hill'

17 Follow signs for Shepperdine. After 10 km (6 miles), at T-j R 'The River, The Windbound'. Fine views of estuary.

18 Retrace route for 200 m (yd), then follow signs for Shepperdine

19 At T-j R 'Oldbury 1¼, Thornbury 3½'

20 At X-roads SA 'Oldbury Village'

21 At T-j R 'Oldbury, Cowhill'. Through Oldbury (The Anchor PH)

◀ previous page

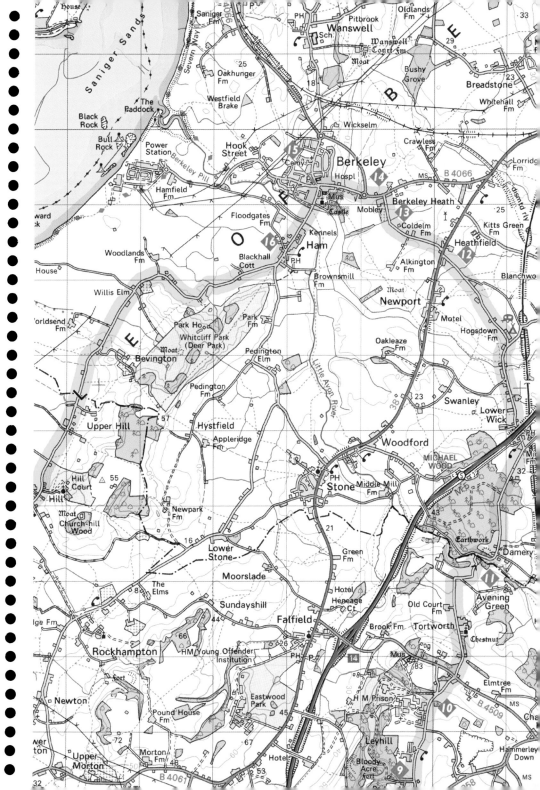

Easy Cotswold riding west of Malmesbury

The route for this easy ride takes in the two prosperous Cotswold towns of Malmesbury and Tetbury and several small villages with beautiful stone buildings.

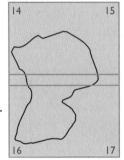

Start

Market cross in the centre of Malmesbury

P Long-term car parks can be found by taking the B4040 Bristol road out of the centre of Malmesbury and following signs for New Station car park

Distance and grade

44 km (28 miles)

Easy

Terrain

Rolling or flat, no serious hills

Nearest railway

Kemble, 8 km (5 miles) north of Malmesbury

Refreshments

Suffolk Arms PH♥♥, *plenty of choice in* **Malmesbury**
Vine Tree PH♥♥, **Norton**
The Crown PH♥, **Tetbury**
Plenty of choice in **Sherston**
Star Inn, Queens Head PH, **Hullavington**

Malmesbury

Tetbury

Sherston

Malmesbury 1

Positioned on the upper reaches of the Avon, this is the oldest borough in England. It owes its prosperity to the weaving industry that flourished in the 15th century, and many weavers' houses built of Cotswold stone can still be seen. The market cross that dates from 1490 is one of the finest in England.

Malmesbury Abbey 1

This great abbey made the town famous with its foundation in the 7th century. A major part of the later Norman building survives today. The richly carved south porch is particularly outstanding and a musician's gallery is situated above the nave arcade.

▲ Market Hall, Tetbury

Tetbury 3

Pre-historic Tetbury was the site of a hill fort later taken by the Romans. Through the Middle Ages it prospered as a wool and yarn market selling wool from the Cotswold hill sheep. The pillared Elizabethan market hill is thought to have been the place where local merchants brought their wool to be weighed. Fine merchants' houses and craftsmens' cottages remain and there is a variety of restaurants, tea rooms and specialist shops.

Westonbirt Arboretum 6

Internationally famous, the arboretum has one of the finest and largest collections of trees in the world. Managed by the Forestry Commission since 1956, it has some 17,000 trees and shrubs.

Alderton

Grittleton

Hullavington

Foxley

1 With back to the Market Cross R towards the church, abbey and a large traffic mirror (!). At T-j by memorial cross R past Three Cups PH. Follow signs for Tetbury through three roundabouts, bearing L onto the B4014 at the third

2 Bear L again at T-j, following signs for Tetbury. This is the one stretch of the ride where you are not on quiet lanes, which start near Tetbury, so **take care**

3 In Tetbury bear R at the Market Hall 'Dursley, Stroud'

4 After 400 m (yd), L on the A4135 'Dursley, Stroud'

5 After 1 km (¾ mile), on RH bend, L 'Leighterton 4'

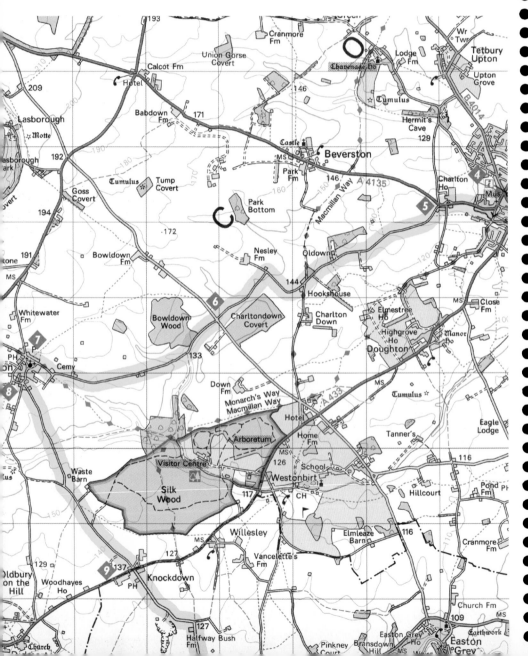

6 SA at X-roads 'Leighterton'

7 Immediately after Royal Oak PH in Leighterton L 'Knockdown 2, Didmarton 2'

8 Soon after PH bear L, passing church on left, then at X-roads L 'Knockdown 2'

9 At X-roads with A433 SA 'Sherston 2'

two pages

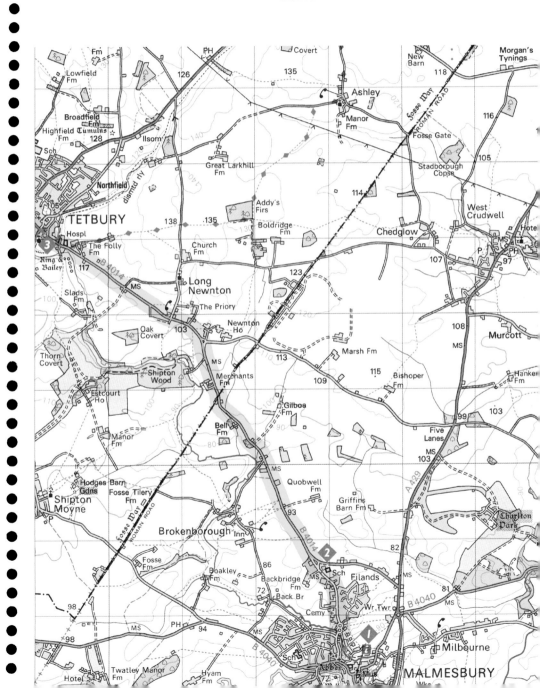

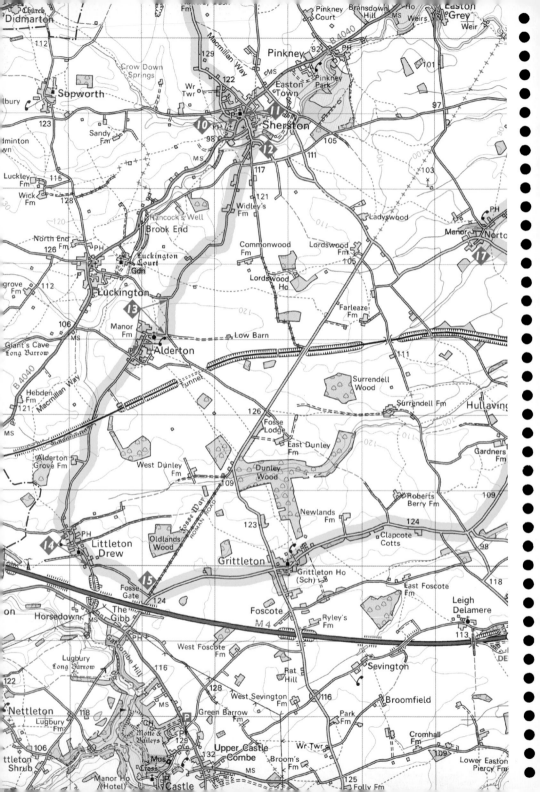

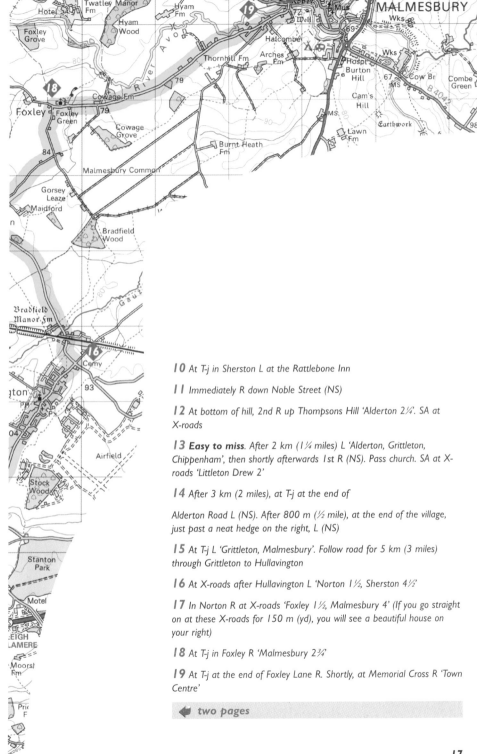

10 At T-j in Sherston L at the Rattlebone Inn

11 Immediately R down Noble Street (NS)

12 At bottom of hill, 2nd R up Thompsons Hill 'Alderton 2¼'. SA at X-roads

13 **Easy to miss**. After 2 km (1¼ miles) L 'Alderton, Grittleton, Chippenham', then shortly afterwards 1st R (NS). Pass church. SA at X-roads 'Littleton Drew 2'

14 After 3 km (2 miles), at T-j at the end of

Alderton Road L (NS). After 800 m (½ mile), at the end of the village, just past a neat hedge on the right, L (NS)

15 At T-j L 'Grittleton, Malmesbury'. Follow road for 5 km (3 miles) through Grittleton to Hullavington

16 At X-roads after Hullavington L 'Norton 1½, Sherston 4½'

17 In Norton R at X-roads 'Foxley 1½, Malmesbury 4' (If you go straight on at these X-roads for 150 m (yd), you will see a beautiful house on your right)

18 At T-j in Foxley R 'Malmesbury 2¾'

19 At T-j at the end of Foxley Lane R. Shortly, at Memorial Cross R 'Town Centre'

⬅ **two pages**

3 Easy Cotswold riding east of Malmesbury

The route east of Malmesbury provides an easy ride through small villages and along quiet lanes. It crosses the River Avon twice before climbing out of the valley at Little Somerford and continuing east towards the lovely woods of Somerford Common – a good place for a picnic. Should you wish someone else to prepare your lunch for you, the Wheatsheaf Inn in Oaksey is a fine country pub.

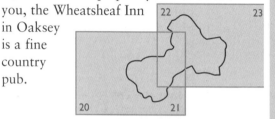

22   23

20   21

Start

Market cross in the centre of Malmesbury

P Long-term car parks can be found by taking the B4040 Bristol road out of the centre of Malmesbury and following signs for New Station car park

Distance and grade

46 km (29 miles)

Easy

Terrain

Rolling or flat, no serious hills

Nearest railway

Kemble, 8 km (5 miles) north of Malmesbury

▶ Malmesbury Abbey

Malmesbury   Corston   Startley   Great Somerford   Little Somerford

Places of interest

Malmesbury 1

Many famous names are associated with Malmesbury: St Aldhelm (656–709); King Athelstan, who gave the town its royal heath; William of Malmesbury, a great historian of the Middle Ages and the philosopher Thomas Hobbes (1588–1679).

Refreshments

Volunteer Inn, **Great Somerford**
Little Somerford Arms PH,
Little Somerford
Turnpike Arms PH, **Minety**
Horse and Groom PH 🍺**, Charlton**
Three Crowns PH 🍺🍺**, Brinkworth**
The Wheatsheaf PH 🍺**, Oaksey**

Elmer of Malmesbury – the Flying Monk

In 1010 AD, Elmer, a Saxon monk, climbed to the top of Malmesbury Abbey Tower and attempted to fly with the wings he had made. This flight lasted more than 190 m (620 ft), but on landing he broke both legs. A window in the abbey recalls this event.

Oaksey 15

On the border with Gloucestershire, the parish contains Norwood Castle, a Norman earthwork scheduled as an ancient monument. The village has Tudor and 17th-century houses and the church has some interesting 15th-century wall paintings uncovered in 1933.

Minety   Upper Minety   Oaksey   Charlton

1 With back to the Market Cross R towards the church, abbey and a large traffic mirror (!). At T-j by Memorial Cross L 'Sherston B4040'

2 1st L, 'Foxley 2, Norton 3½'. Cross bridge over River Avon. Climb hill and bear L after 400 m (yd) 'Common Road to Corston'

3 After 3 km (2 miles), at T-j with A429 R, then L opposite Radnor Arms PH on to Rodbourne Road. **Take care!** This is a busy road and it may be best to cross the road and push your bike along the pavement for 200 m (yd) as far as Rodbourne Road

4 Shortly after passing octagonal communications tower on your left in Rodbourne, next R 'Rodbourne Bottom, Cleeve House'. At T-j with Oakdene Cottage opposite R

5 After 1 km (¾ mile), 1st L in Startley 'Great Somerford 1¼, Dauntsey 3½'

6 At X-roads in Great Somerford L 'Little Somerford, Malmesbury'

7 After 2½ km (1½ miles) at T-j in Little Somerford L then immediately R onto Clay Street

8 At T-j with main road (B4042) R 'Swindon 13', then L 'Cleverton, Minety'

➡ **three pages**

19 At T-j (with B4040) in Charlton at the end of Vicarage Lane R 'Malmesbury'

20 Through village. Shortly after the end of the houses, before a signposted RH bend turn L 'Garsdon 1, Lea 1½'

21 After 1 km (¾ mile) at X-roads (your priority) R 'Malmesbury'

22 After 2 km (1¼ miles) on sharp RH bend by a telephone box bear L (in effect SA) onto No Through Road 'Wiltshire Cycleway'

23 At A429 SA on to Blicks Lane

24 At T-j opposite Duke of York PH L into Malmesbury

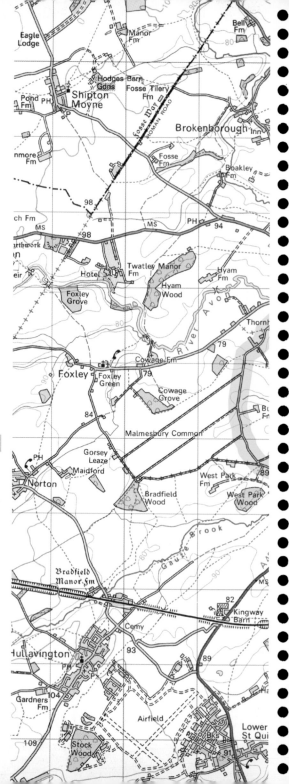

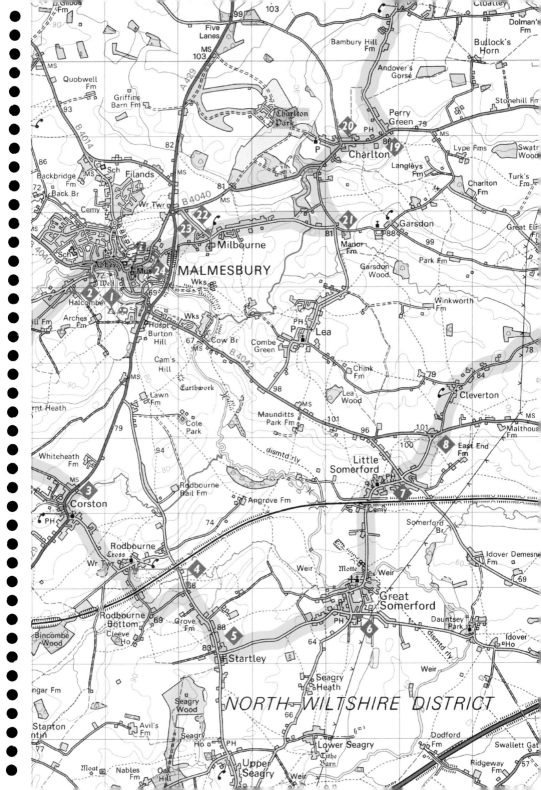

8 At T-j with main road (B4042) R 'Swindon 13', then L, 'Cleverton, Minety'

9 At T-j R 'Brinkworth, Wootton Bassett'

10 At T-j L 'Minety 3½'

11 At offset X-roads R then L 'Minety 2½, Purton 4½'

12 At T-j L 'Minety'

13 At X-roads with B4040 SA into Minety

14 After almost 3 km (2 miles), on gentle LH bend in Upper Minety, R 'Minety Church, Oaksey 2'

15 At X-roads in Oaksey SA for the Wheatsheaf Inn or L 'Crudwell, Culkerton, Malmesbury' to continue route

16 At mini-roundabout by Post Office at the end of Oaksey village 'Eastcourt'

17 At X-roads SA 'Hankerton, Charlton, Malmesbury'

18 At T-j L 'Hankerton, Charlton'

19 At T-j (with B4040) in Charlton at the end of Vicarage Lane R 'Malmesbury'

20 Through village. Shortly after the end of the houses, before a signposted RH bend turn L 'Garsdon 1, Lea 1½'

21 After 1 km (¾ mile) at X-roads (your priority) R 'Malmesbury 2'

◀ **three pages**

From Clifton to Clevedon, west of Bristol

To explore one of Bristol's best escapes into the countryside, begin by crossing the Avon Gorge via the Clifton Suspension Bridge; after 1½ km (1 mile) on the A369, you plunge into a network of small country lanes that lead to the impressive church at Lower Failand with good views across to the Bristol Channel.

A swift descent down a narrow lane brings you to Portbury and the start of the section along the Gordano Valley.

About 8 km (5 miles) on from Portbury, the route climbs out of the valley and up onto the ridge between Portishead and Clevedon, with fine views out across the Bristol Channel to Wales.

Continue across Clevedon Moor and Kenn Moor gathering strength on this flat section for the major climb of the ride up through the thickly wooded Brockley Combe.

The final stage of the ride takes you through Long Ashton and Ashton Court, a pleasant way to regain height back up to the suspension bridge.

Start

Clifton Suspension Bridge, west of Bristol

P Towards or on the Downs, north of the Bridge

Distance and grade

51 km (32 miles)
Moderate

Terrain

Mainly undulating, through a variety of scenery. One long hill, 130 m (430 ft) over 5 km (3 miles) up onto Lulsgate and three short steep ones (before Failand, before Clevedon, and after Barrow Gurney)

Nearest railway

Bristol Temple Meads. Alternatively, Yatton is 5 km (3 miles) from the route at Kenn Moor

Refreshments

Black Horse PH, **Clapton in Gordano**
Plenty of choice in **Clevedon**
Blue Flame PH, **West End** *(east of Clevedon)*
Princes Motto PH, **Barrow Gurney**

Clifton Suspension Bridge | Failand | Portbury | Clapton | Clevedon

Places of interest

Clifton Suspension Bridge 1
The distinctive landmark stands 74 m (245 ft) above high water and has a total span of 210 m (702 ft). Work started on the bridge in 1836, based on a design by Isambard Kingdom Brunel but it was not officially opened until 1864. The most famous story concerning the bridge is that of Sarah Ann Henley. In 1885 she jumped off the bridge after a quarrel with her lover and was gently parachuted by her petticoats to the mud below.

Avon Gorge Nature Reserve 2
Leigh Woods is a beautiful woodland owned by the National Trust. The gorge is cut out of limestone and is famous for rare trees and flowers.

Clevedon 12
A quiet seaside town that has retained much of its earlier Victorian charm, Clevedon lies on a part of the Bristol Channel known for its high tides, which caused the pier to collapse in 1970.

Clevedon Court 16
This 14th-century manor house was once fortified and is one of the oldest of its type to have survived anywhere in Britain. It is still the home of the Elton family whose outstanding collection of family portraits, 19th-century Eltonware pottery and Nailsea glass are on show.

Short cuts

For a 21 km (13 mile) ride at instruction 8, just before Clapton-in-Gordano, L instead of R, cross the bridge over the M5 and climb steeply to the B3128 and B3129 to return via Failand to the suspension bridge

For a 35 km (22 mile) ride go as far as Clevedon, but at instruction 16 go SA and return directly via Tickenham and Failand, taking the B3130, B3128 and B3129

Extensions

After Clevedon, between instructions 17 and 18, take the 1st R and head for the Mendips via Yatton, Wrington and Burrington

After crossing the A38 near Lulsgate, after instruction 21 and before 22, follow the Avon Cycleway from Felton via Chew Stoke, Pensford, Compton Dando to Saltford to return to Bristol via the Bristol and Bath Cyclepath. If you need to return to the suspension bridge, you will have to cross the centre of Bristol. This longer ride is about 80 km (50 miles)

Clevedon Craft Centre and Countryside Museum 16
Situated in the grounds of Clevedon Court. Here you can watch the craftsmen at work in a rural atmosphere. There are over 12 studios with high-quality crafts for sale and a tea room for refreshments.

Barrow Gurney

Long Ashton

1 Cross the suspension bridge, at T-j with A369 R 'Abbots Leigh, Clevedon'. **Take care** on this 1½-km (1-mile) stretch of A-road

2 SA at traffic lights. After pelican crossing 1st L on Manor Road just before George PH

3 1st R down Manor Lane. After 400 m (yd) L at junction of roads

4 Climb to Failand church, then 1st R on Failand Lane 'Portbury 1½'

5 At T-j after long descent R 'Portbury, Portishead'

6 At bottom of hill on sharp RH bend L on High Street 'Portbury, Clapton, Nailsea'

7 After 100 m (yd) L on Caswell Lane 'Clapton, Nailsea'

8 At T-j by 'Give Way' sign after 3 km (2 miles) at the end of Caswell Lane R then L after 300 m (yd) onto Clevedon Lane 'Clapton Wick, Clevedon'

➡️ *next page*

20 At X-roads with A370 SA on to Brockley Combe Road. 130 m (430 ft) climb over 5 km (3 miles). This section may be busy (up to 5 cars per minute)

21 After 5 km (3 miles), at T-j with A38 L then 1st R 'Felton, Winford'

22 200 m (yd) after last houses in Felton L on Raglan Lane (**easy to miss**) then R at T-j with Vee Lane

23 At T-j with more major road (B3130) L (NS)

24 At A38 SA at X-roads onto Hobbs Lane '6'0" width limit'

25 Bear R towards end of lane, then at X-roads with B3130 SA onto Wild Country Lane

26 At top of short steep hill, at T-j bear L (in effect SA) 'Long Ashton'

27 At T-j R on Weston Road through Long Ashton to junction with B3128

28 SA into Ashton Court through gateway. After 200 m (yd), sharply L to continue uphill to Lodge by A369

29 SA A369 to return to suspension bridge

8 At T-j by 'Give Way' sign after 3 km (2 miles) at the end of Caswell Lane R then L after 300 m (yd) onto Clevedon Lane 'Clapton Wick, Clevedon'

9 After 6½ km (4 miles), at T-j with B3124, R on Walton Road 'Walton, Portishead'

10 After 300 m (yd) 1st L 'Walton St. Mary' up Holly Lane, which becomes Castle Road then Wellington Terrace

11 800 m (½ mile) after the Highcliffe Hotel and opposite church with red tile roof on the left bear R down Marine Parade 'Seafront'

12 At T-j at the end of the promenade (The Beach) R on Elton Road

13 Bear L along Old Church Road. At traffic lights SA past shops to clock tower

14 Bear L, past more shops onto Old Street

15 At roundabout after 1½ km (1 mile) R on B3130 'Nailsea'. Next roundabout SA to B3130 'Nailsea'

16 After 300 m (yd) 1st R onto Court Lane 'Clevedon Craft Centre'

17 1 km (¾ mile) after Craft Centre at X-roads by Give Way sign L

18 **Ignore** 1st R on Kenn Moor Road. 1½ km (1 mile) after passing Blue Flame PH on your left take next R '7.5 ton weight limit'

19 Cross railway bridge and pass church on the left. Next R onto Brockley Lane (sign may be obscured by brambles). Follow signs for Brockley Combe

20 At X-roads with A370 SA on to Brockley Combe Road (130 m (430 ft) climb over 5 km (3 miles)). This section may be busy (up to 5 cars per minute)

◀ *previous page*

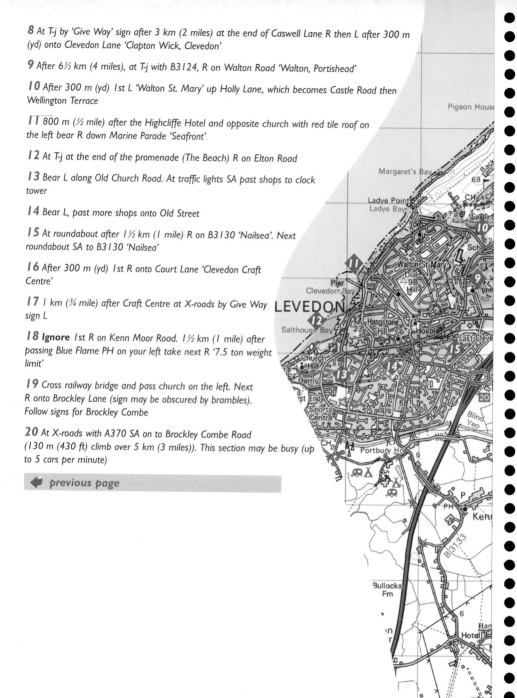

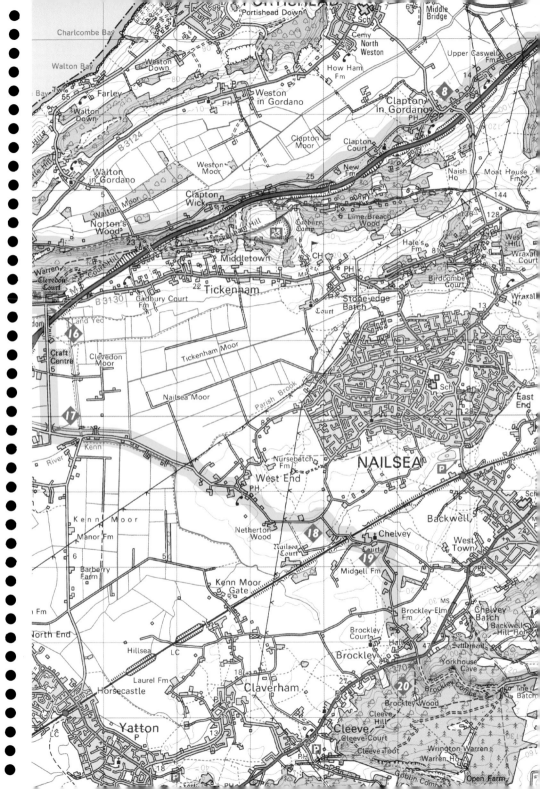

Bath to Castle Combe and Lacock

The ride out of Bath beside the Kennet and Avon canal to the east takes you along the beautiful towpath to Bathampton then climbs out of the valley into the southern Cotswolds via Marshfield before dropping down to the delights of Castle Combe. Another climb takes you south and east to the equally fascinating village of Lacock. Skirting south of Corsham, the ride climbs steadily to Kingsdown, with magnificent views towards Bath, before dropping into Bathford and a return along the towpath.

Start

Bath Spa railway station

🅿 If arriving by car, it is better to start and finish at Bathampton, near the George PH and do the route from instructions 5 to 35

Distance and grade

56 km (35 miles)
🔥🔥🔥 Moderate

Terrain

Two climbs of 150 m (500 ft), a steep one from Batheaston to Marshfield and a more steady one from Lacock to Kingsdown. Apart from these and two short steep hills near Castle Combe, the ride is generally flat or undulating

Nearest railway

Bath Spa

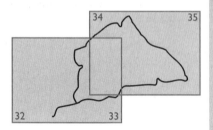

Bath　Batheaston　Marshfield　Mountain Bower　Castle Combe

Bath 1

The famous Roman baths were built around the natural hot spring, which rises from the ground at 46.5°C. The presence of the spring established Bath as a bathing, curative and social centre and remained fashionable in the 18th century. Bath is also famous for its elegant Georgian architecture. The Royal Crescent, the first terrace to be built as a crescent, remains as one of the finest examples in Europe. Bath also has numerous museums, a magnificent abbey and an industrial heritage centre.

Lacock 23

A National Trust village of stone and half-timbered houses dating back to the 15th century with none later than 1800.

Lacock Abbey 23

The magnificent Lacock Abbey standing on the banks of the River Avon was founded in 1232 by the Countess of Salisbury. The original cloisters and chapter house survive, but after its supression in 1539, it was converted into a Tudor dwelling house by Sir William Sharrington.

The Fox Talbot Photographic Museum 23

The museum is situated in a 16th-century barn near the gates of Lacock Abbey. It displays the work and equipment of WH Fox Talbot, a pioneer of photography who once owned the abbey.

 Refreshments

The George PH 🍷🍷, Plenty of choice in **Lacock**
Lord Nelson PH 🍷, Catherine Wheel PH 🍷🍷,
Marshfield
Plenty of choice in **Castle Combe**

Castle Combe 15

A picturesque village in the wooded Bybrook valley of Cotswold stone houses with a stone-canopied marked cross at the centre. The village was the venue for the film *Doctor Dolittle* in 1966.

Kennet and Avon Canal 3 and 36

Opened by the Queen in 1990, the canal stretches 137 km (87 miles) between Reading and Bristol passing through 104 locks and over a height of 140 m (450 ft).

Lacock   Gastard   Chapel Plaister

1 L out of station, past car hire office, through tunnel to rear of station

2 Walk bike across green bridge over river, L on Rossiter Road

3 After 50 m (yd) L 'Thimble Mill Conference and Banqueting Suite'. Do not cross bridge. Go immediately R alongside canal

4 Follow signs 'Bathampton, Kennet and Avon Canal Towpath' for 3 km (2 miles), crossing bridges and changing sides as indicated by signs. This will involve some short flights of steps. You are advised to dismount under the bridges where the path is narrow

5 At George PH leave canal, L over railway bridge then tollbridge over Avon, passing Old Mill Hotel

6 At T-j R. **Take care** crossing road

7 After 800 m (½ mile), shortly after the White Hart PH ignore left turn on 'The Batch'. Take the next L up Penthouse Hill 'North End, St Catherine'

8 Follow this road for 2½ km (1½ miles) ignoring R and L turns until signpost 'Oakford, Marshfield, Colerne'. R downhill to cross stream

9 Long climb, steep at the end. At T-j at the top of Oakford Lane L

10 After 4 km (2½ miles) at T-j at the end of St Martins Lane in Marshfield turn R, following High Street around LH then RH bend to emerge at A420

11 At T-j with A420 R for 800 m (½ mile) then 1st L 'West Kington, Nettleton'

➡ **three pages**

30 Go down steep hill. At X-roads SA A365 (NS)

31 At T-j by Hatt Farm R. Follow past golf course down into Kingsdown

32 At T-j by Crown PH R on A361 towards railway bridge. Just before bridge, L on footpath (push bike until railway crossing)

33 Fork R up over railway bridge to cross river

34 Over stile, cross field diagonally R to next stile, then with great care SA railway crossing

35 On tarmac track to The George PH at Bathampton. L opposite primary school

36 Retrace route to Bath, following signs 'Kennet and Avon Canal Towpath Bath'

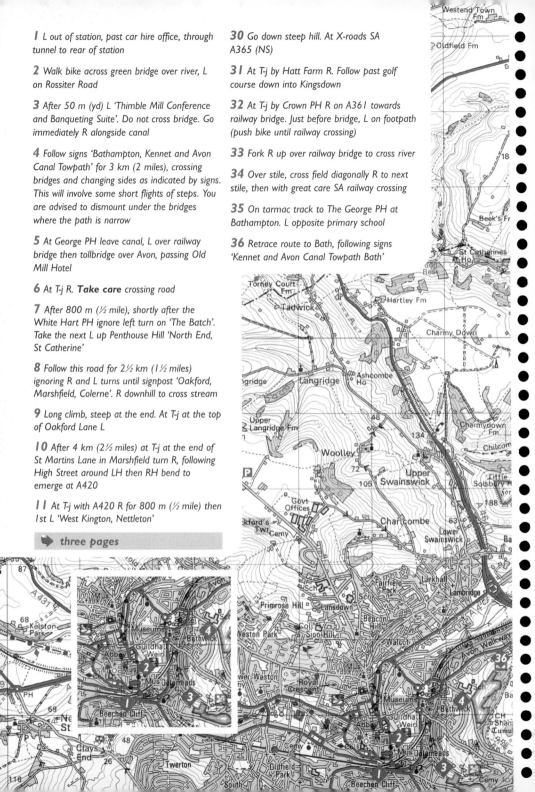

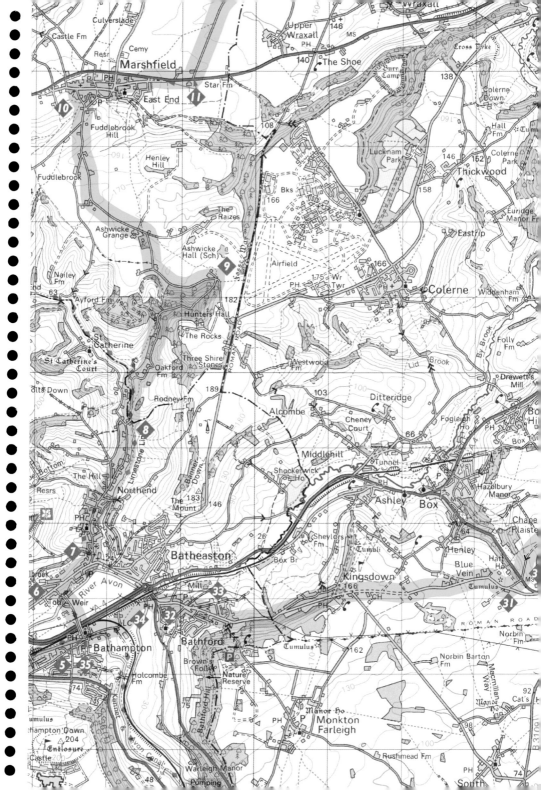

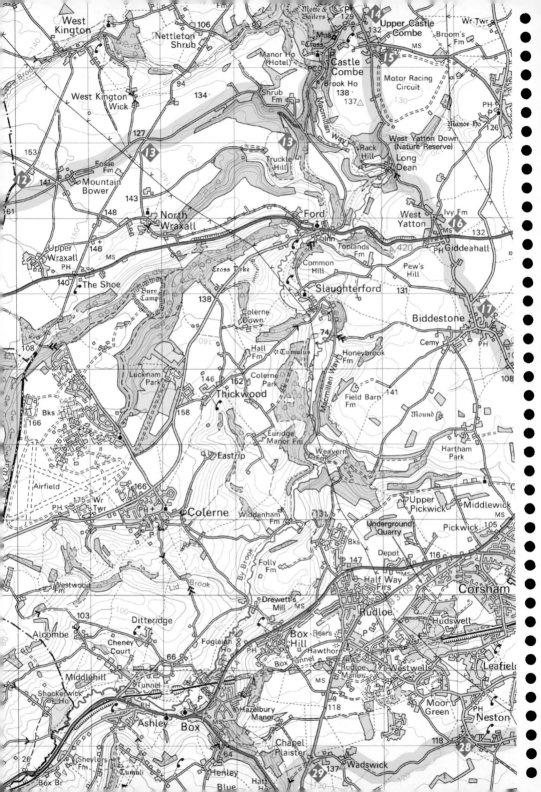

12 After 1½ km (1 mile) 1st R 'Mountain Bower'. At X-roads SA 'Nettleton, Castle Combe'

13 At 2nd X-roads SA 'Castle Combe'. At T-j sharply L downhill (NS)

14 Through Castle Combe up steady hill to T-j with B4039. R 'Chippenham'

15 After 400 m (¼ mile), on sharp LH bend, R (in effect SA) 'West Yatton, Giddeahall'

16 After 3 km (2 miles), at X-roads with the A420 by The Crown cross the grass verge SA to get to the lane opposite

17 At T-j R 'Corsham'. Through Biddestone past pubs. Ignore left turn on Chippenham Lane. Take next L after 400 m (¼ mile) by a triangle of grass

18 At X-roads SA 'Lacock'

19 At next X-roads, with A4, SA 'Easton, Notton, Lacock, Melksham' – **take care**

20 Keep following signs for Lacock. 20 m (yd) **before** T-j with A350 R (NS)

21 At T-j on Corsham Road L for 100 m (yd) to A350

22 At T-j R then immediately L into Lacock, joining the Wiltshire Cycleway

23 50 m (yd) past George Inn, on sharp LH bend, R (in effect SA) 'Melksham, Devizes, Trowbridge'

24 At small roundabout R then immediately R again along Folly Lane 'no through road'

25 **Take care** crossing busy A350. SA to continuation of Folly Lane 'Gastard'

26 After 3 km (2 miles) at T-j by Harp and Crown PH R 'Corsham, Bath'

27 1st L at X-roads down Monks Lane. 'The Ridge' 'RN Store Depot Monks Park'

28 Follow road through Neston following signs for West Wells, then Chapel Plaister

29 At large triangle of grass planted with trees just before main road bear L to T-j on B3109. L then immediately R (NS)

three pages

River valleys and canals near Marlborough

Starting from the attractive and prosperous town of Marlborough with its plethora of eating and drinking establishments, the ride heads southwest. It leaves the Kennet valley, crossing the ridge along which the old Wansdyke earthworks run, with fine views across the Vale of Pewsey into which it descends. The lovely village of Great Bedwyn with its most unusual post office is the start of the second climb back into the Kennet valley at Ramsbury; from here the ride follows the river back to Marlborough.

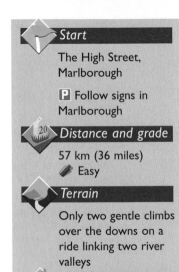

Start

The High Street, Marlborough

P Follow signs in Marlborough

Distance and grade

57 km (36 miles)

Easy

Terrain

Only two gentle climbs over the downs on a ride linking two river valleys

Nearest railway

Great Bedwyn (on the route itself)

Refreshments

Bruce Arms PH, **Easton Royal**
Cross Keys PH, **Great Bedwyn**
Bell Inn, **Ramsbury**
Royal Oak PH, **Wootton Rivers**
Plenty of choice in **Pewsey**
Plenty of choice in **Marlborough**
Seven Stars PH, **Woodborough**
Red Lion PH, **Axford**

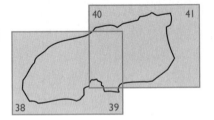

Marlborough   Lockeridge   Woodborough   Pewsey   Wootton Rivers

Marlborough 1

Merlin, the magician of King Arthur's court, was, according to legend, buried under the town's castle mound. A noticeable feature of Marlborough is the Georgian High Street; one of the widest streets in the country, this was once one of the most important staging posts on the London to Bath road, now the A4. It is a reminder of the old town, much of which was destroyed or damaged by fires or the Civil War.

Pewsey 7

Famous for the White Horse, overlooking the town, that was cut in 1937 to commemorate the coronation of King George VI.

Ramsbury 21

In Saxon times, Ramsbury was the centre of a flourishing diocese with a cathedral and bishop but for nine centuries now it has been no more than a parish.

▲ Marlborough

Crofton   Great Bedwyn   Ramsbury   Axford

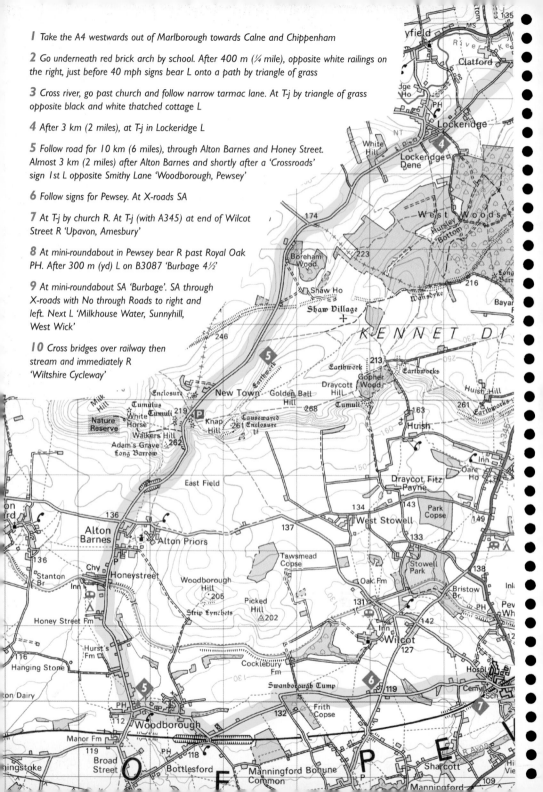

1 Take the A4 westwards out of Marlborough towards Calne and Chippenham

2 Go underneath red brick arch by school. After 400 m (¼ mile), opposite white railings on the right, just before 40 mph signs bear L onto a path by triangle of grass

3 Cross river, go past church and follow narrow tarmac lane. At T-j by triangle of grass opposite black and white thatched cottage L

4 After 3 km (2 miles), at T-j in Lockeridge L

5 Follow road for 10 km (6 miles), through Alton Barnes and Honey Street. Almost 3 km (2 miles) after Alton Barnes and shortly after a 'Crossroads' sign 1st L opposite Smithy Lane 'Woodborough, Pewsey'

6 Follow signs for Pewsey. At X-roads SA

7 At T-j by church R. At T-j (with A345) at end of Wilcot Street R 'Upavon, Amesbury'

8 At mini-roundabout in Pewsey bear R past Royal Oak PH. After 300 m (yd) L on B3087 'Burbage 4½'

9 At mini-roundabout SA 'Burbage'. SA through X-roads with No through Roads to right and left. Next L 'Milkhouse Water, Sunnyhill, West Wick'

10 Cross bridges over railway then stream and immediately R 'Wiltshire Cycleway'

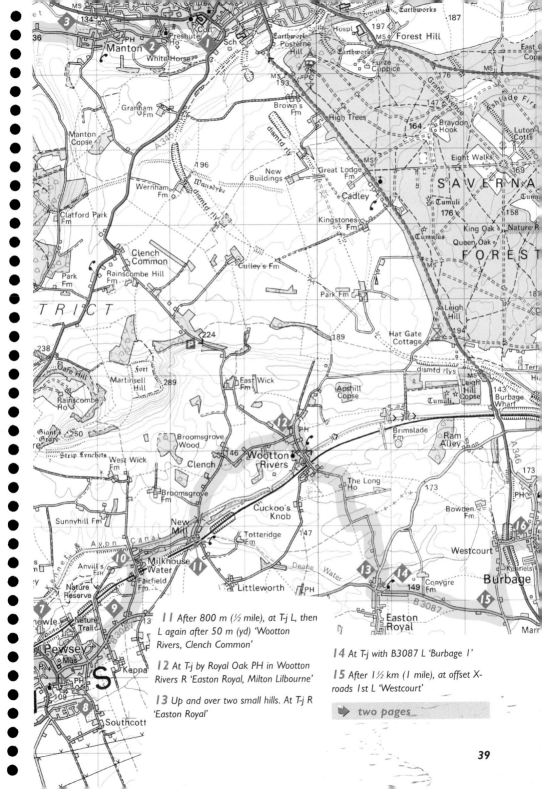

11 *After 800 m (½ mile), at T-j L, then L again after 50 m (yd) 'Wootton Rivers, Clench Common'*

12 *At T-j by Royal Oak PH in Wootton Rivers R 'Easton Royal, Milton Lilbourne'*

13 *Up and over two small hills. At T-j R 'Easton Royal'*

14 *At T-j with B3087 L 'Burbage 1'*

15 *After 1½ km (1 mile), at offset X-roads 1st L 'Westcourt'*

➡ **two pages**

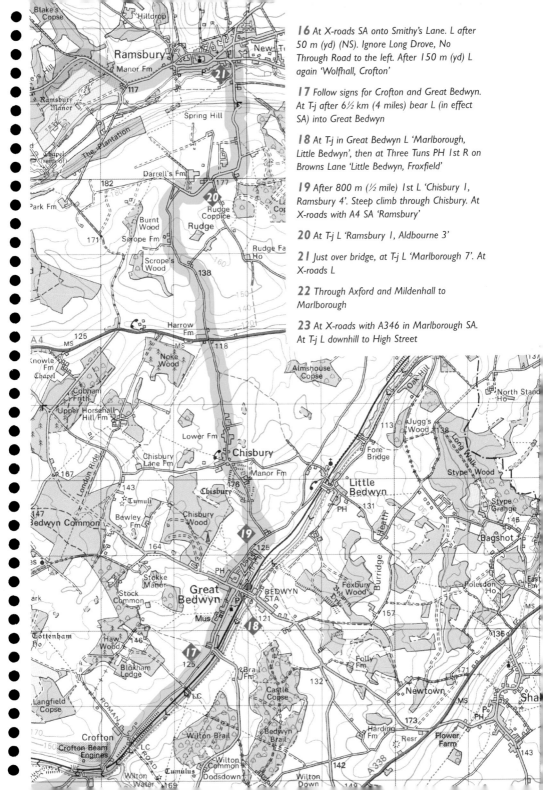

16 At X-roads SA onto Smithy's Lane. L after 50 m (yd) (NS). Ignore Long Drove, No Through Road to the left. After 150 m (yd) L again 'Wolfhall, Crofton'

17 Follow signs for Crofton and Great Bedwyn. At T-j after 6½ km (4 miles) bear L (in effect SA) into Great Bedwyn

18 At T-j in Great Bedwyn L 'Marlborough, Little Bedwyn', then at Three Tuns PH 1st R on Browns Lane 'Little Bedwyn, Froxfield'

19 After 800 m (½ mile) 1st L 'Chisbury 1, Ramsbury 4'. Steep climb through Chisbury. At X-roads with A4 SA 'Ramsbury'

20 At T-j L 'Ramsbury 1, Aldbourne 3'

21 Just over bridge, at T-j L 'Marlborough 7'. At X-roads L

22 Through Axford and Mildenhall to Marlborough

23 At X-roads with A346 in Marlborough SA. At T-j L downhill to High Street

Over the Lambourn Downs and down into the Vale of White Horse

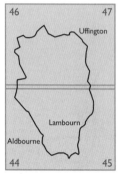

The Lambourn Downs are criss-crossed with gallops for training race horses, and the plethora of bridleways in the area is good news for off-road cyclists Man's influence in the area, however, far pre-dates the training of horses; indeed, the region contains more signs of prehistoric civilization than almost anywhere else in the British Isles. The route climbs to the edge of the Downs, crossing the Ridgeway close to Uffington Castle and Whitehorse Hill. Both Kingston Lisle and Uffington have many attractive stone and thatch cottages. A short, flat section in the Vale of White Horse and through Shrivenham leaves you at the edge of the chalk escarpment in Bishopstone. The Ridgeway is crossed a second time, and the old Roman Road, the Ermin Way, is joined for a couple of miles before a descent into the charming village of Aldbourne. There is a last, steep climb over Marridge Hill before a fast descent drops you back in the square in Lambourn.

Start

The Red Lion PH in the centre of Lambourn

P On the High Street (B4000) south out of Lambourn towards Hungerford

Distance and grade

51 km (32 miles)

Moderate

Terrain

Three climbs: 70 m (230 ft) to the Ridgeway north of Lambourn, 91 m (300 ft) from Bishopstone to Shepherds Rest PH and 91 m (300 ft) from Aldbourne to Coppington Down above Lambourn

Nearest railway

Hungerford, 10 km (6 miles) south of Lambourn

Lambourn   Kingston Lisle   Uffington   Shrivenham   Bourton

Lambourn 1

Lambourn is a centre for racehorse training, with miles of specially prepared gallops on the surrounding downland. King Alfred is said to have chosen Lambourn for a palace. It also boasts a 12th-century church and 16th-century almshouses ranged around a flowered court.

Aldbourne 16

The majestic church of St Michael is a conglomeration of all kinds of periods from Norman onwards. The interior presents a vivid picture of Aldbourne's history with numerous monuments to the Walrond and Goddard families. Also in the church are a pair of 18th-century fire engines, known affectionately as Adam and Eve; they served the village well through several major fires, the last in 1921. Around the square are a number of fine Georgian houses that recall the village's importance as a centre for bell-founding and the weaving of fustian.

▲ *Whitehorse Hill, The Manger*

Bishopstone Shepherds Rest PH Aldbourne Preston Membury

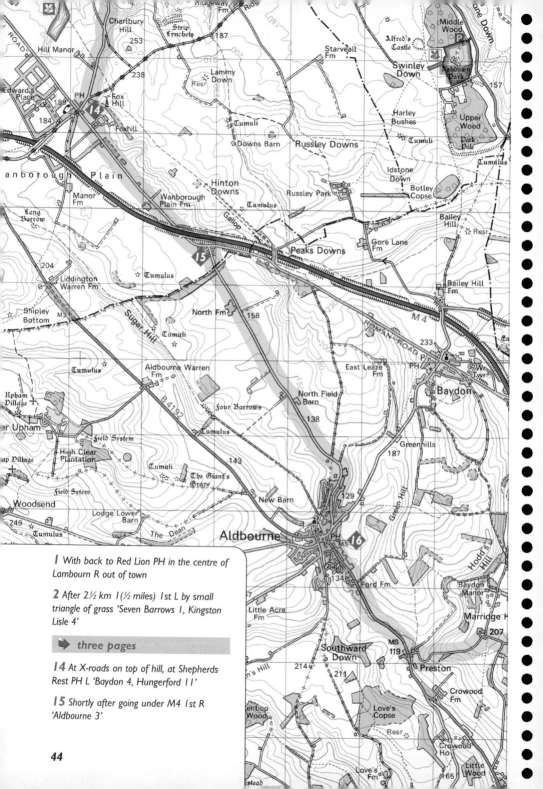

1 With back to Red Lion PH in the centre of Lambourn R out of town

2 After 2½ km 1 (½ miles) 1st L by small triangle of grass 'Seven Barrows 1, Kingston Lisle 4'

➡ **three pages**

14 At X-roads on top of hill, at Shepherds Rest PH L 'Baydon 4, Hungerford 11'

15 Shortly after going under M4 1st R 'Aldbourne 3'

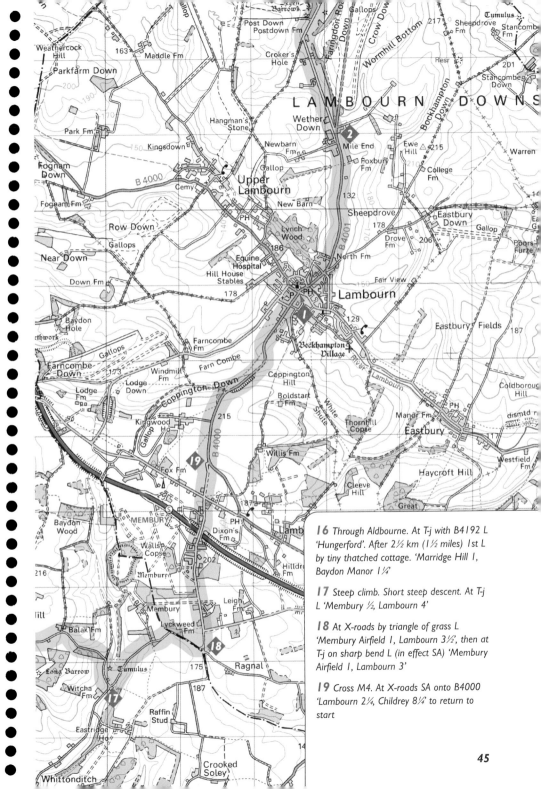

16 Through Aldbourne. At T-j with B4192 L 'Hungerford'. After 2½ km (1½ miles) 1st L by tiny thatched cottage. 'Marridge Hill 1, Baydon Manor 1¼'

17 Steep climb. Short steep descent. At T-j L 'Membury ½, Lambourn 4'

18 At X-roads by triangle of grass L 'Membury Airfield 1, Lambourn 3½', then at T-j on sharp bend L (in effect SA) 'Membury Airfield 1, Lambourn 3'

19 Cross M4. At X-roads SA onto B4000 'Lambourn 2¼, Childrey 8¼' to return to start

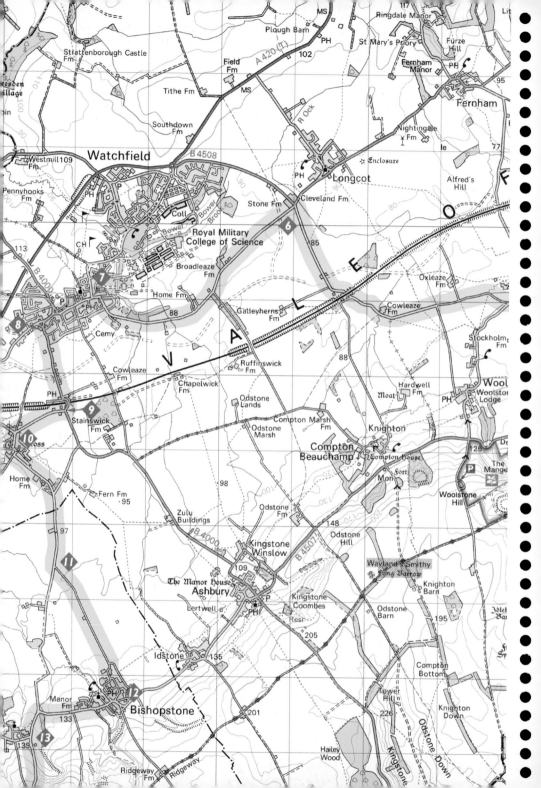

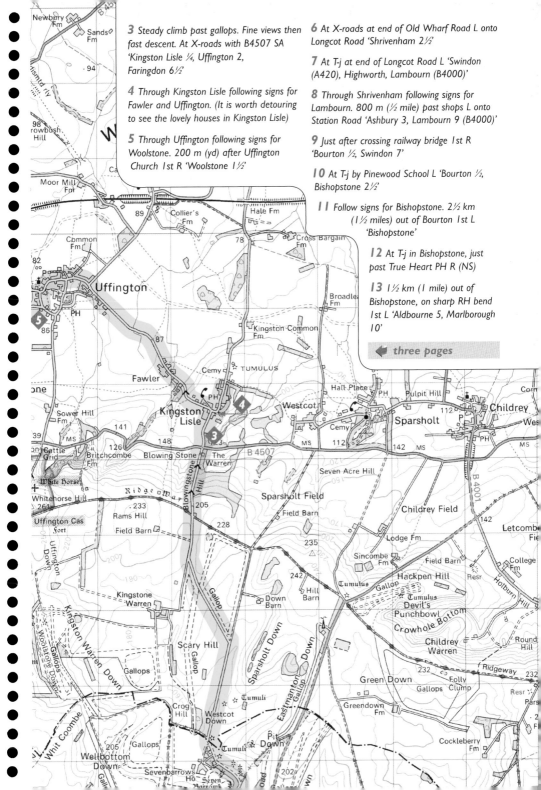

3 Steady climb past gallops. Fine views then fast descent. At X-roads with B4507 SA 'Kingston Lisle ¼, Uffington 2, Faringdon 6½'

4 Through Kingston Lisle following signs for Fawler and Uffington. (It is worth detouring to see the lovely houses in Kingston Lisle)

5 Through Uffington following signs for Woolstone. 200 m (yd) after Uffington Church 1st R 'Woolstone 1½'

6 At X-roads at end of Old Wharf Road L onto Longcot Road 'Shrivenham 2½'

7 At T-j at end of Longcot Road L 'Swindon (A420), Highworth, Lambourn (B4000)'

8 Through Shrivenham following signs for Lambourn. 800 m (½ mile) past shops L onto Station Road 'Ashbury 3, Lambourn 9 (B4000)'

9 Just after crossing railway bridge 1st R 'Bourton ½, Swindon 7'

10 At T-j by Pinewood School L 'Bourton ½, Bishopstone 2½'

11 Follow signs for Bishopstone. 2½ km (1½ miles) out of Bourton 1st L 'Bishopstone'

12 At T-j in Bishopstone, just past True Heart PH R (NS)

13 1½ km (1 mile) out of Bishopstone, on sharp RH bend 1st L 'Aldbourne 5, Marlborough 10'

three pages

From Cirencester along the edge of the Golden Valley and on to Withington

The numerous straight roads emanating from Cirencester are evidence of the fact that it once was a Roman town, Corinium. In general, these are now main roads and of little interest to the cyclist. The route heads south from here, then west to the very edge of the Golden Valley along which the River Frome and the Stroudwater Canal run. There are superb views from between Frampton Mansell and Sapperton. Easy riding takes you north through the villages of Winstone and Elkstone before you encounter the hills and valleys formed by the River Churn, Hilcot Brook and the River Coln at Withington. One last climb takes you to the top of the ridge where you feel as though you are on the roof of the Cotswolds as you begin your long, gentle descent back into Cirencester.

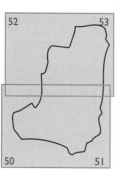

 Start

Tourist Information Centre, Cirencester

P Several long-stay car parks on the outskirts of the town

 Distance and grade

54 km (34 miles)

Moderate (short route options are easy grade)

 Terrain

Essentially flat or undulating except at the northern end near Withington where there are 3 hills of 61 m (200 ft), 85 m (280 ft) and finally 91 m (300 ft) to climb onto the northern end of the White Way. The latter drops gently over 11 km (7 miles) into Cirencester

 Nearest railway

Kemble

Cirencester

Ewen

Tarlton

Frampton Mansell

Sapperton

Cirencester 1

Corinium Dobunorum was the name of this Roman town that became the second largest in England. When the Romans withdrew, Cirencester declined but its strategic position at the confluence of the major routeways, Fosse Way, Ermin Way and Akeman Street, combined with its vast sheep pastures brought it

▼ *Cirencester*

great wealth in the Middle Ages. Money from the wool paid for the Church of St John the Baptist, one of the largest of its kind in the country. Other places of interest in the town are:

Corinium Museum

An impressive collection of Roman remains clearly displayed to relate to the development of the Cotswolds from the earliest times with special reference to the Roman period.

Cirencester Workshops

Located at Brewery Court in the town, this Victorian brewery has been converted and houses a range of craft workshops including leatherworkers, textiles, bookbinders and a blacksmith. There is a gallery showing exhibitions and a wholefood coffee house.

Refreshments

Slug & Lettuce PH ❧, plenty of choice in **Cirencester** *Wild Duck PH ❧❧,* **Ewen** *Thames Head PH ❧,* **Kemble** *(just east of instruction 8) Tunnel House PH ❧❧, just north of* **Tarlton** *(instruction 9) Crown PH ❧,* **Frampton Mansell** *Bell PH ❧❧,* **Sapperton** *Colesbourne Inn ❧,* **Colesbourne** *The Mill PH ❧,* **Withington**

Duntisbourne Abbots 14

This village stands at the head of a beautiful wooded valley.

Miserden Park 14

Shrubs, roses, perennial borders, topiary and spring bulbs in a picturesque woodland setting.

Withington 22

A pretty village in the Coln Valley that has an unusually large church as its focal point.

Winstone Elkstone Withington White Way

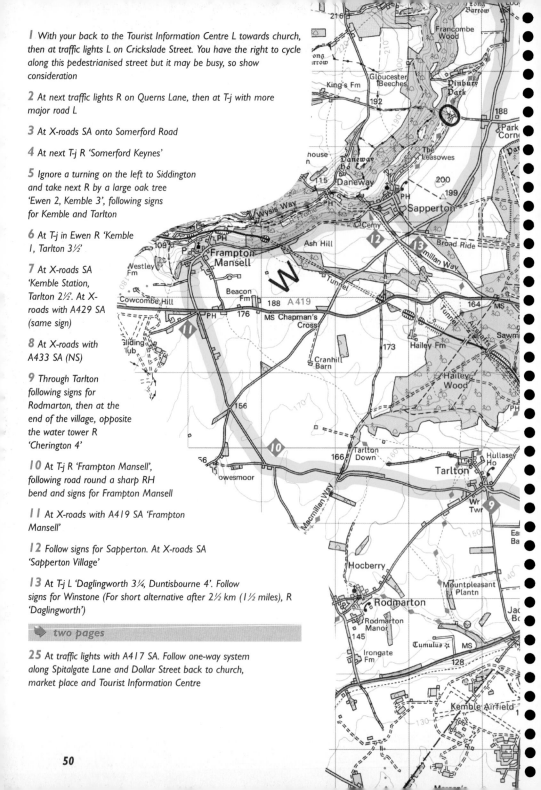

1 With your back to the Tourist Information Centre L towards church, then at traffic lights L on Cricklade Street. You have the right to cycle along this pedestrianised street but it may be busy, so show consideration

2 At next traffic lights R on Querns Lane, then at T-j with more major road L

3 At X-roads SA onto Somerford Road

4 At next T-j R 'Somerford Keynes'

5 Ignore a turning on the left to Siddington and take next R by a large oak tree 'Ewen 2, Kemble 3', following signs for Kemble and Tarlton

6 At T-j in Ewen R 'Kemble 1, Tarlton 3½'

7 At X-roads SA 'Kemble Station, Tarlton 2½'. At X-roads with A429 SA (same sign)

8 At X-roads with A433 SA (NS)

9 Through Tarlton following signs for Rodmarton, then at the end of the village, opposite the water tower R 'Cherington 4'

10 At T-j R 'Frampton Mansell', following road round a sharp RH bend and signs for Frampton Mansell

11 At X-roads with A419 SA 'Frampton Mansell'

12 Follow signs for Sapperton. At X-roads SA 'Sapperton Village'

13 At T-j L 'Daglingworth 3¼, Duntisbourne 4'. Follow signs for Winstone (For short alternative after 2½ km (1½ miles), R 'Daglingworth')

two pages

25 At traffic lights with A417 SA. Follow one-way system along Spitalgate Lane and Dollar Street back to church, market place and Tourist Information Centre

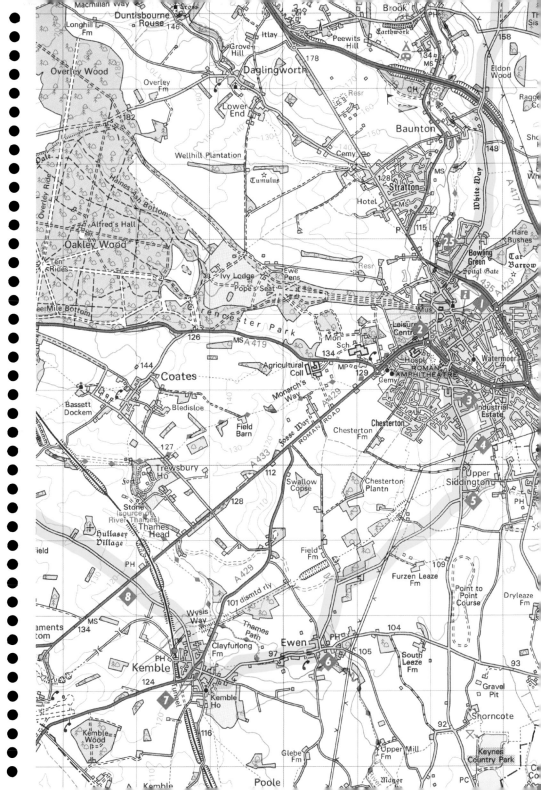

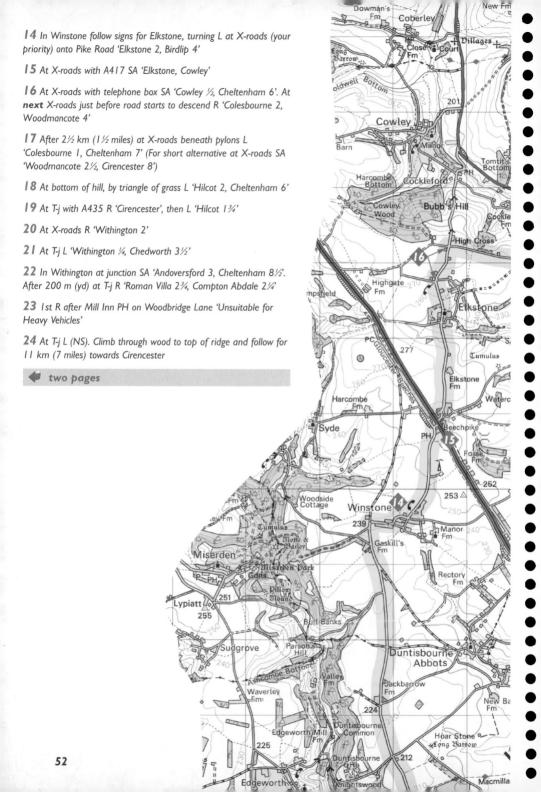

14 In Winstone follow signs for Elkstone, turning L at X-roads (your priority) onto Pike Road 'Elkstone 2, Birdlip 4'

15 At X-roads with A417 SA 'Elkstone, Cowley'

16 At X-roads with telephone box SA 'Cowley ½, Cheltenham 6'. At **next** X-roads just before road starts to descend R 'Colesbourne 2, Woodmancote 4'

17 After 2½ km (1½ miles) at X-roads beneath pylons L 'Colesbourne 1, Cheltenham 7' (For short alternative at X-roads SA 'Woodmancote 2½, Cirencester 8')

18 At bottom of hill, by triangle of grass L 'Hilcot 2, Cheltenham 6'

19 At T-j with A435 R 'Cirencester', then L 'Hilcot 1¾'

20 At X-roads R 'Withington 2'

21 At T-j L 'Withington ¼, Chedworth 3½'

22 In Withington at junction SA 'Andoversford 3, Cheltenham 8½'. After 200 m (yd) at T-j R 'Roman Villa 2¾, Compton Abdale 2¼'

23 1st R after Mill Inn PH on Woodbridge Lane 'Unsuitable for Heavy Vehicles'

24 At T-j L (NS). Climb through wood to top of ridge and follow for 11 km (7 miles) towards Cirencester

← **two pages**

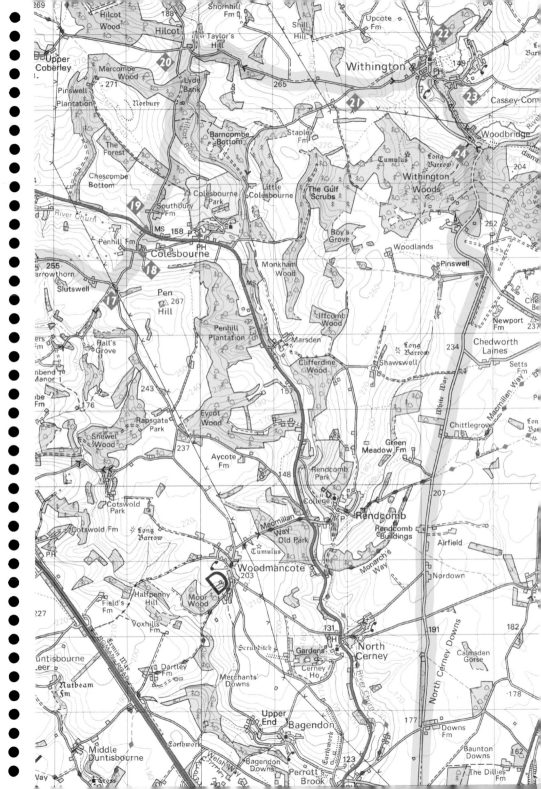

Very easy riding in the Severn Vale around Frampton on Severn

9

Here is an ideal ride or series of short rides for people who want to start cycling or take it up again. It is also suitable for more experienced cyclists who do not need the challenge of the

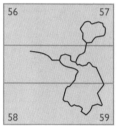

Cotswold escarpment and simply want to enjoy the quiet lanes and river views of this tucked-away corner of the Severn Vale. Starting from the spacious village of Frampton on Severn, the ride heads westwards right to the banks of the Severn at Arlingham Passage, with fine views across to the Forest of Dean. You would have to travel over 48 km (30 miles) by road to get to Newnham, the village that is just a few hundred yards away on the other side of the river. Returning eastwards, you have a choice of finishing after this first loop of 16 km (10 miles) and going back to Frampton or heading north and doing the second loop via Longney and Elmore. A detour to the river at Weir Green is worthwhile just to see how much smaller it has become in a few miles. The third loop crosses to the other side of the M5 as far as Frocester, with the Cotswolds looming ahead, before returning via Cambridge and Slimbridge and a short spell on the Gloucester and Sharpness Canal towpath back to Frampton.

The third loop uses a short section of the canal towpath. You will need a permit from the British Waterways Board and can apply for one at www.britishwaterways.co.uk or by calling 01923-201120.

Start

The Green, Frampton on Severn

P Small car park by the post office, Frampton on Severn

Distance and grade

16, 19 and 19 km (10, 12 and 12 miles) (three loops total 54 km (34 miles)

Easy

Terrain

Flat

Nearest railway

Stonehouse, 3 km (2 miles) from the route at Frocester or Gloucester, 6½ km (4 miles) from the route at Elmore

Frampton on Severn   Arlingham   Overton   Longney   Elmore

Frampton on Severn

The village green at Frampton on Severn covers more than 20 acres. It is fringed by a number of Georgian houses including Frampton Court, which is a grade I Vanbrugh House and family home. Frampton Manor stands at the other side of the green, a timber-framed house with a walled garden that is said to be the birthplace of 'Fair Rosamund' Clifford, a mistress of Henry II.

 Refreshments

The Bell PH, **Frampton on Severn**
Red Lion PH, Old Passage Inn, **Arlingham**
The Ship Inn, **Saul** Anchor Inn, **Epney**
Queen Victoria PH, Kings Head PH, **Eastington**
Royal Gloucestershire Hussars PH, **Frocester**

▲ The Gloucester and Sharpness canal

Longney   Whitminster   Eastington   Frocester   Cambridge

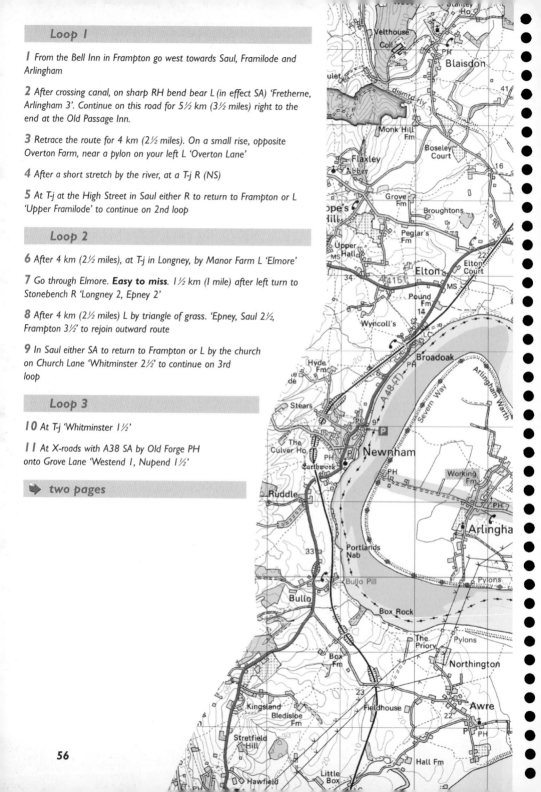

Loop I

1 From the Bell Inn in Frampton go west towards Saul, Framilode and Arlingham

2 After crossing canal, on sharp RH bend bear L (in effect SA) 'Fretherne, Arlingham 3'. Continue on this road for 5½ km (3½ miles) right to the end at the Old Passage Inn.

3 Retrace the route for 4 km (2½ miles). On a small rise, opposite Overton Farm, near a pylon on your left L 'Overton Lane'

4 After a short stretch by the river, at a T-j R (NS)

5 At T-j at the High Street in Saul either R to return to Frampton or L 'Upper Framilode' to continue on 2nd loop

Loop 2

6 After 4 km (2½ miles), at T-j in Longney, by Manor Farm L 'Elmore'

7 Go through Elmore. **Easy to miss**. 1½ km (1 mile) after left turn to Stonebench R 'Longney 2, Epney 2'

8 After 4 km (2½ miles) L by triangle of grass. 'Epney, Saul 2½, Frampton 3½' to rejoin outward route

9 In Saul either SA to return to Frampton or L by the church on Church Lane 'Whitminster 2½' to continue on 3rd loop

Loop 3

10 At T-j 'Whitminster 1½'

11 At X-roads with A38 SA by Old Forge PH onto Grove Lane 'Westend 1, Nupend 1½'

➡ **two pages**

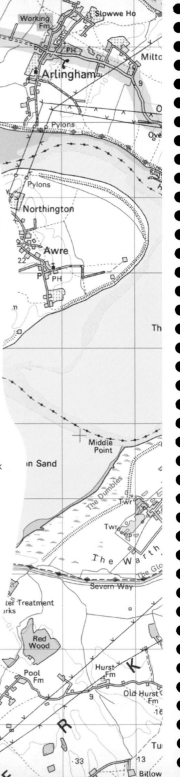

Loop 1

1 From the Bell Inn in Frampton go west towards Saul, Framilode and Arlingham

2 After crossing canal, on sharp RH bend bear L (in effect SA) 'Fretherne, Arlingham 3'. Continue on this road for 3½ miles right to the end at the Old Passage Inn.

3 Retrace the route for 2½ miles. On a small rise, opposite Overton Farm, near a pylon on your left L 'Overton Lane'

4 After a short stretch by the river, at a T-j R (NS)

5 At T-j at the High Street Saul either R to return to Frampton or L 'Upper Framilode' to continue on 2nd loop at instruction 6

Loop 3

10 At T-j L 'Whitminster 1½'

11 At X-roads with A38 SA by Old Forge PH (NS)

12 At roundabout with A419 SA 'Eastington 1'

13 At roundabout at the end of Eastington L 'Frocester, Bath'

14 At X-roads in Frocester by Royal Gloucestershire Hussars PH R 'Coaley 2,

15 At T-j shortly after going under railway bridge R 'Cam 3, Dursley 4'

16 400 m (yd) after going under railway bridge a second time, 1st R opposite letter box (NS)

17 At T-j L through lay-by onto A38, then R just past the George Inn onto Ryalls Lane (NS)

18 Follow this SA through 'no through road' sign and over canal bridge

19 R along towpath, recrossing canal at 1st (white) bridge and following road back into Frampton

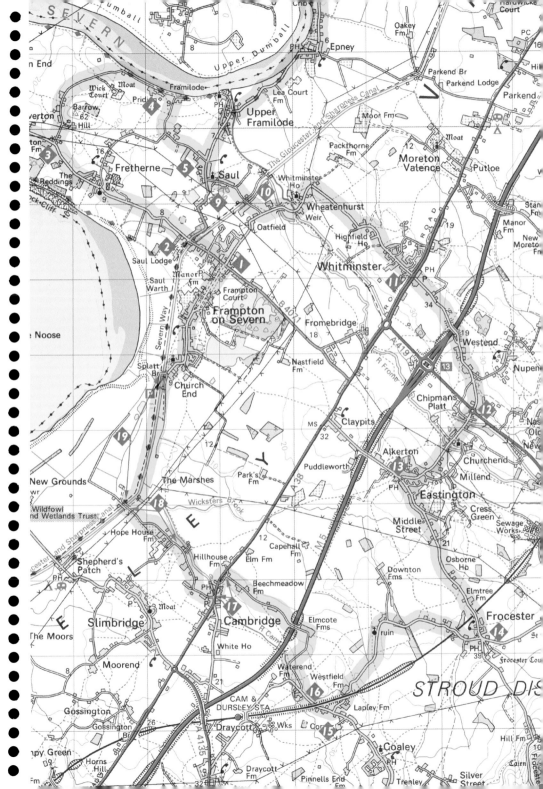

From Wotton-under-Edge to the River Severn, returning via Uley

You will find this a ride of contrasts, with some very easy riding in the Vale of Severn and two hard climbs, one at the start and one near the end. The route avoids the busy B4060 north of Wotton by climbing Wotton Hill and dropping via Waterley Bottom to North Nibley, providing wide views out towards the river. Three points of interest in the Vale of Berkeley are Berkeley Castle, the Gloucester and Sharpness Canal and The Wildfowl Trust at Slimbridge. The hills beckon and the route weaves its way between Cam Long Down, Uley Bury and Downham Hill before dropping into Uley. You now face the real test: Bencome Hill, 146 m (480 ft) of climbing in a mile. The return to Wotton uses a road that is busier than one might normally choose but the rewards are not only magnificent views right at the edge of the escarpment near the golf course but also a thrilling descent back down to the start.

Start

Wotton-under-Edge

P Small car park following signs for Hillesley and Alderley

Distance and grade

48 km (30 miles)

Moderate/strenuous

Terrain

A short, sharp 91 m (300 ft) climb at the start onto Wotton Hill. Descent to Severn Vale for easy cycling. The climb back onto the Cotswolds is split into two: a gradual then steeper climb from the Vale to Uley; a much longer, steeper hill from Uley to the A4135 143 m (470 ft)

Nearest railway

Stonehouse, 6½ km (4 miles) from Coaley

Refreshments

Plenty of choice in **Wotton-under-Edge**
New Inn P 🍺🍺, **Waterley Bottom** (just north of instruction 4) Black Horse PH 🍺, **North Nibley** Plenty of choice in **Berkeley** The Salmon PH 🍺, **Wanswell** Berkeley Arms PH 🍺, Berkeley Hunt Inn, **Purton** Tudor Arms PH 🍺, **Shepherd's Patch** (just west of instruction 18) Old Crown PH 🍺, **Uley**

Wotton-under-Edge / Wotton Hill — North Nibley — Berkeley — Wanswell — Purton — Halmore

Wotton-under-Edge

A market town with 17th- and 18th-century houses. Isaac Pitman (1813-1897) inventor of shorthand was born in Orchard Street.

Berkeley 11

A quiet Georgian town dominated by the castle, Berkeley also has a fine Early English church, which contains many memorials to the Berkeley family. The churchyard contains the grave of Edward Jenner (1749-1823) pioneer of smallpox vaccination who was born here.

▲ *Uley Bury*

Berkeley Castle 11

Situated south of the town of Berkeley, this Norman fortress, built in the reign of Henry II, has been transformed into a magnificent stately home surrounded by Elizabethan terraced gardens. It has been the ancestral home of the Berkeley family for over 800 years. A butterfly farm set in a walled garden houses many species of exotic and British butterflies.

Hetty Pegler's Tump 22

A Neolithic Long Barrow where 38 skeletons have been found. It is 36 m by 6 m (120 by 22 ft) with 4 chambers.

Uley Bury 23

This commanding Iron Age fort is a superb vantage point with deep ramparts covering 32 acres.

Slimbridge   Cambridge   Coaley   Uley   A4135

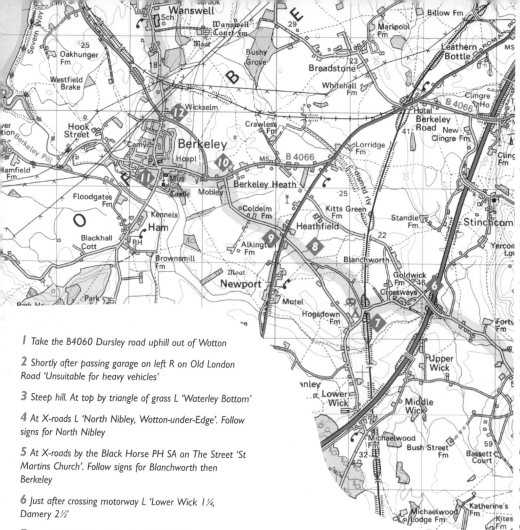

1 Take the B4060 Dursley road uphill out of Wotton

2 Shortly after passing garage on left R on Old London Road 'Unsuitable for heavy vehicles'

3 Steep hill. At top by triangle of grass L 'Waterley Bottom'

4 At X-roads L 'North Nibley, Wotton-under-Edge'. Follow signs for North Nibley

5 At X-roads by the Black Horse PH SA on The Street 'St Martins Church'. Follow signs for Blanchworth then Berkeley

6 Just after crossing motorway L 'Lower Wick 1¼, Damery 2½'

7 Immediately after railway bridge 1st R (there may be grass growing in the road!)

8 At T-j R (NS)

9 At T-j with A38 R 'Gloucester', then L 'Sharpness 3½'

10 At T-j with B4066 L 'Berkeley ½, Sharpness 4'. At roundabout SA

11 In Berkeley follow road round to the R onto Marybrook Street 'Sharpness'

12 At roundabout SA 'Wanswell 1'

➡ two pages

22 Follow road through Coaley and Hamshill. At the end of Far Green, on sharp RH bend, bear L (in effect SA) uphill 'Uley'

23 At fork in road bear R down Fop Street 'Dursley'

24 At X-roads SA 'Stoutshill, Kingscote 2½, Tetbury 7½'

25 Steep climb. At X-roads with B4058 R 'Wotton 3½, Dursley 3½'

26 At T-j with A4135 R, then at junction after 400 m (yd) bear L 'Wotton' to return to start via wonderful downhill

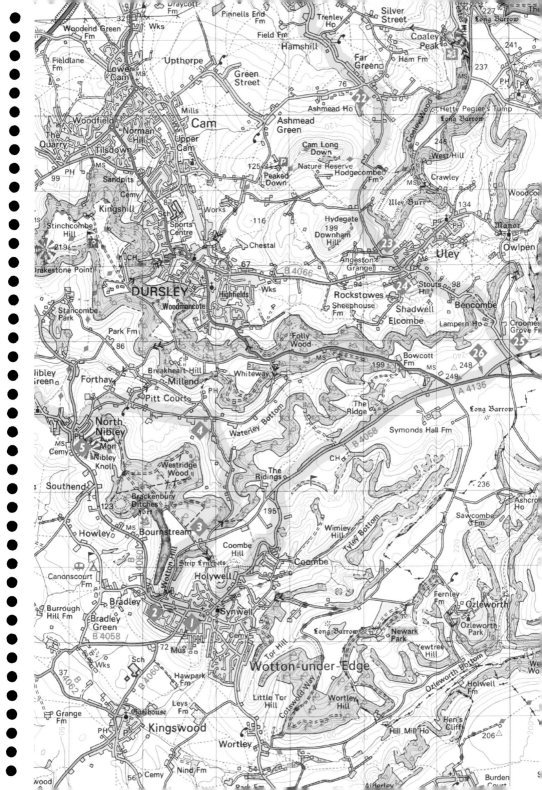

10 At T-j with B4066 L 'Berkeley ½, Sharpness 4'. At roundabout SA

11 In Berkeley follow road round to R onto Marybrook Street 'Sharpness'

12 At roundabout SA 'Wanswell 1'

13 Shortly after the Salmon Inn PH in Wanswell ignore the 1st right to Halmore and Breadstone. On a sharp LH bend after 150 m (yd) take the next R 'Purton, Brookend'

14 In Purton either L over bridge for Berkeley Hunt Inn or Berkeley Arms Inn and river views or follow road around into Halmore

15 **Easy to miss**. At end of Halmore, opposite red-brick Halmore Cottage L 'Gossington, Slimbridge'

16 **Easy to miss**. Shortly after Old Hurst Farm Guest House L on Moorend Lane 'Slimbridge'

17 At T-j with St John's Road L 'Slimbridge, Severn Wildfowl Trust 1½'

18 At end of Slimbridge opposite long red-brick barn R on Longaston Lane 'Troytown'

19 At T-j with Ryalls Lane R

20 At T-j with A38 L then R just past George PH into lay-by and 1st R

21 At T-j opposite the interesting buildings of Coaley Mill L (NS)

22 Follow road through Coaley and Hamshill. At the end of Far Green, on sharp RH bend bear L (in effect SA) uphill 'Uley'

◀ **three pages**

East from Abergavenny to Raglan

Abergavenny is in many ways the gateway to the Welsh mountains from the east. It is surrounded by three distinctively shaped hills: the Skirrid, the Blorenge and the Sugar Loaf, and during the course of the ride there are fine views of all three and of many others besides. You start climbing right from the beginning of the ride and then descend to run parallel with the noisy A40 for a brief stretch before Raglan. A visit to the well-preserved, atmospheric castle in Raglan is highly recommended. The old A40 (now a yellow road) is surprisingly busy, hence the twists and turns to avoid it west of Raglan. Three climbs to the north and then to the west take you back up onto the rolling hills near Llantilio Crossenny and Cross Ash with magnificent views opening up. The ridge ride up over Campston Hill is particularly memorable. A fast descent to Llanivangel Crucorney takes you past an excellent old pub. The last gentle climb to Pantygelli sets you up for a fine, exhilarating descent down into Abergavenny.

Start

The Baptist Church / War Memorial at the end of the High Street, Abergavenny

P Large, free car park on the central ring road, opposite super-markets, close to the start

Distance and grade

48 km (30 miles)

Moderate

70   71

Aberga venny

68   69

Abergavenny (Y Fenni)   Llanddewi Rhydderch   Pit   Great Oak   Bryngwyn

Terrain

Four main climbs –
120 m (400 ft) climb at
the start east from
Abergavenny, 120 m
(400 ft) climb north
from Llantilio
Crossenny, 91 m
(300 ft) climb near
Cross Ash with one
steep section, 85 m
(280 ft) climb to the
highpoint on Campston
Hill. Lowest point –
50 m (165 ft) in
Abergavenny and
Raglan. Highest point –
270 m (900 ft) at the
top of Campston Hill,
northeast of
Llanivangel Crucorney

Nearest railway

Abergavenny

Refreshments

Hen & Chickens PH 🍺, *plenty of choice in* **Abergavenny**
(Clytha Arms PH 🍺🍺, west of **Raglan**, *instruction 8)*
Ship PH 🍺, *plenty of choice in* **Raglan**
Hostry Inn, **Llantilio Crossenny**
Three Salmons PH, *near* **Cross Ash**
Skirrid Inn 🍺🍺, **Llanivangel Crucorney**
Crown PH, **Pantygelli**

Places of interest

Abergavenny 1
Spectacular mountain ranges surround
this market town on the River Usk. The
labyrinth of narrow streets, some with
Tudor buildings, testifies to the town's
long history, linked to the fortunes of the
ruined 11th-century castle. The castle
now houses a collection of old farming
equipment. The museum in the 19th-
century hunting lodge traces the town's
history

Raglan Castle 12
Romantic ruins of the 15th-century,
moated fortress with a massive hexago-
nal keep, two courtyards and a double-
fronted gatehouse. The surrender of the
castle to Parliamentarians in 1646
marked the end of the Civil War

White Castle 14 (2½ km (1½ miles) off the route)
Ruined, moated castle on a windswept
hilltop, one of the 'Three Castles of
Gwent' –
a triangle of
fortresses pro-
tecting the border
against the Welsh.
The castle dates
from the 12th century
and was strengthened
by Edward I a century
later

Llantilio
Crossenny

Llanvihangel
Crucorney

67

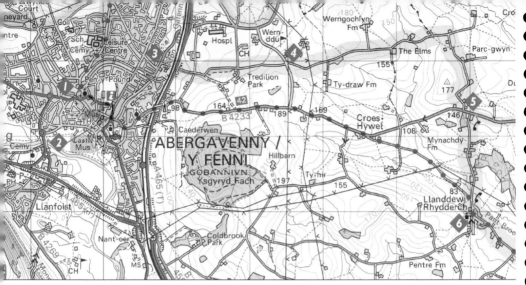

1 With back to the Baptist church L towards Monmouth and Hereford. After 200 m (yd) 1st R opposite car park. At T-j L 'Museum of Childhood' towards Farmers Arms PH

2 At X-roads at the end of Lion Street SA onto Lower Monk Street 'B4233 Rockfield 12, Hospital' then immediately L onto Ross Road

3 At T-j bear R (in effect SA) (NS) then shortly 1st R onto Tredilion Road

4 Climb. At X-roads by pylons SA past Tredilion Fruit Farm

5 At T-j (with B4233) L then 1st R. (For short cut, do not take the 1st R but continue SA and rejoin route at Llantilio Crossenny, instruction 14)

6 At T-j bear L through Llandewi Rhydderch. After 2 km (1¼ miles) at the top of short hill R 'Penpergwm'. Fast descent

7 After 1 km (¾ mile) as road swings sharp right 1st L (NS)

8 At T-j near to the bridge over the A40 L then 1st R 'Great Oak 1'

9 Shortly after telephone box and RH bend in Great Oak 1st L (NS). At T-j by triangle of grass R (NS)

▼ The Skirrid Mountain (Ysgyryd Fawr) near Abergavenny

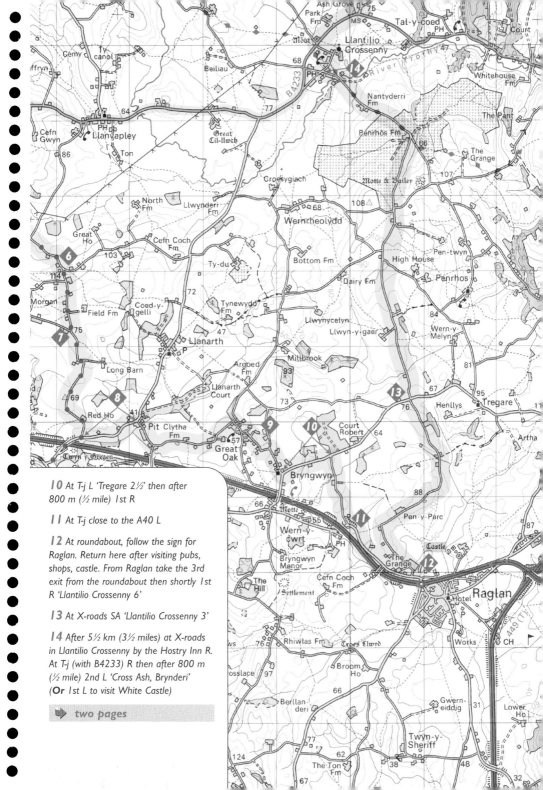

10 At T-j L 'Tregare 2½' then after 800 m (½ mile) 1st R

11 At T-j close to the A40 L

12 At roundabout, follow the sign for Raglan. Return here after visiting pubs, shops, castle. From Raglan take the 3rd exit from the roundabout then shortly 1st R 'Llantilio Crossenny 6'

13 At X-roads SA 'Llantilio Crossenny 3'

14 After 5½ km (3½ miles) at X-roads in Llantilio Crossenny by the Hostry Inn R. At T-j (with B4233) R then after 800 m (½ mile) 2nd L 'Cross Ash, Brynderi' (**Or** 1st L to visit White Castle)

➡ two pages

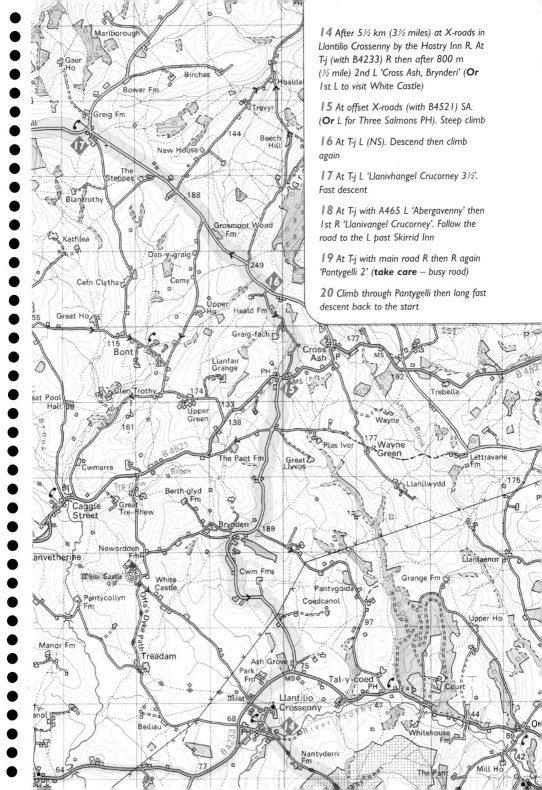

14 After 5½ km (3½ miles) at X-roads in Llantilio Crossenny by the Hostry Inn R. At T-j (with B4233) R then after 800 m (½ mile) 2nd L 'Cross Ash, Brynderi' (**Or** 1st L to visit White Castle)

15 At offset X-roads (with B4521) SA. (**Or** L for Three Salmons PH). Steep climb

16 At T-j L (NS). Descend then climb again

17 At T-j L 'Llanivhangel Crucorney 3½'. Fast descent

18 At T-j with A465 L 'Abergavenny' then 1st R 'Llanivangel Crucorney'. Follow the road to the L past Skirrid Inn

19 At T-j with main road R then R again 'Pantygelli 2' (**take care** – busy road)

20 Climb through Pantygelli then long fast descent back to the start

Into the valleys that lie south and west of Monmouth

The Wye Valley, south of Monmouth, is one of the most spectacular settings for the changing autumn colours. Unfortunately, the main road between Monmouth and Chepstow is far from ideal for cycling. This ride heads west from Monmouth before turning south on a very steep road. You become aware of the challenge ahead as soon as you cross the A40. Magnificent views open up behind you. The route partially descends into the Wye Valley near Tintern (or you may wish to drop down to the valley floor to visit the impressive ruins of Tintern Abbey). From here the route heads west towards Usk, climbing to the high point near Newchurch with views now opening up across the Usk Valley. A fast and furious descent brings you alongside the embankments of the River Usk and into the attractive town of Usk itself with a choice of refreshments. A last highlight is the castle at Raglan, best seen towards the end of the day.

Start

The Green Dragon PH, by the roundabout at the bottom of the Main Street, near to Monnow Bridge in Monmouth

P Follow signs

Distance and grade

56 km (35 miles)

Strenuous

Terrain

Several climbs of 46–76 m (150-250 ft) near the start and from Usk back to Monmouth; two major hills in the middle part of the ride – 210 m (700 ft) south from the A40 through Cwmcarvan, including a very steep section: 170 m (570 ft) from Tintern Cross to the high point near Newchurch. Lowest point – 10 m (35 ft) in the Usk Valley south of Usk. Highest point –

250 m (830 ft) at
Newchurch, west of
Devauden

Nearest railway

Chepstow, 10 km
(6 miles) southeast of
the route at Devauden

▼ *Tintern Abbey from Plumweir Cliff*

Places of interest

Monmouth 1
Elegant buildings of many eras enclose
Agincourt Square, including the early
Georgian Shire Hall. Henry V was born
in the castle in 1387. The adjoining Great
Castle House dates from 1673 and the
fortified Monnow Bridge from the 13th
century. The museum has relics belong-
ing to Lord Nelson

Tintern Abbey 10 *(just off the route)*
One of the finest relics of Britain's
monastic age. There are massive vaulted
and arched remains in the splendid
setting of the Wye Valley. The abbey was
founded in the 12th century by
Cistercian monks, rebuilt in the 13th
century and suppressed by Henry VIII in
1536

Usk 20
Small market town dominated by the
ruins of the 12th-century castle. The
Gwent Rural Life Museum is in the old
Malt Barn. The 13th-century Church of
St Mary has fine medieval woodwork and
a Tudor rood-
screen. The
castle-like build-
ing in Maryport
Street was a county
jail, built in 1841

Refreshments

Punch Bowl PH 🍴🍴*, plenty of choice in* **Monmouth**
Lion Inn, **Trellech**
Parkhouse Tavern PH, **Parkhouse**
Fountain Inn, south of **Parkhouse**
Masons Arms PH, **Devauden**
Greyhound PH, south of **Usk**
Royal PH 🍴🍴*, plenty of choice in* **Usk**

Usk
(Brynbuga)

Raglan

Dingestow

Jingle Street

1 With back to the Green Dragon L. After 200 m (yd) turn L opposite the Britannia PH 'Hotel'

2 Ignore 1st left on Link Road. Take next L by telephone box after 3 km (2 miles) 'Raglan 4½'

3 Cross bridge over A40. At T-j R (NS) then 1st L 'Cwmcarvan 2½'. You will have to climb over the hills on the horizon ahead!

4 Bear R at church in Cwmcarvan 'Hillside 1, Trellech 3'

5 At T-j at the top of very steep section of climb L 'Trellech 2'

6 At T-j at the top of the climb L (NS)

7 At T-j with B4293 R 'Trellech ¼, Chepstow 9 ½'

8 Pass the Lion Inn and church in Trellech. On sharp RH bend bear L (in effect SA) 'Llandogo 2½, Catbrook 2, Tintern 4½'

9 After 800 m (½ mile) fork R by triangle of grass 'Parkhouse 1'. Pass the Fountain Inn and steeply downhill

➡️ *two pages*

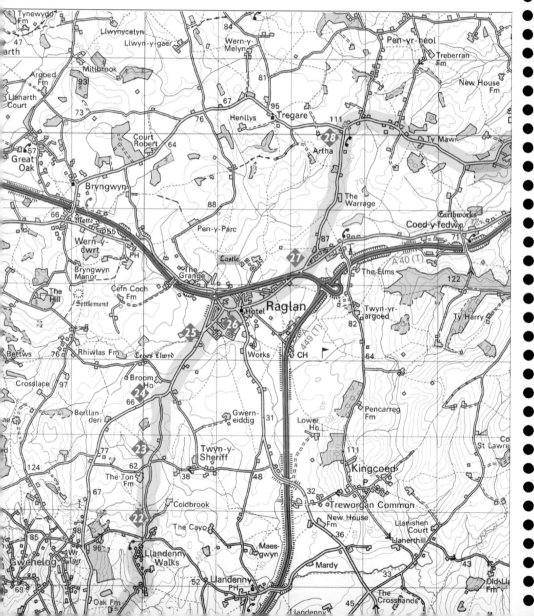

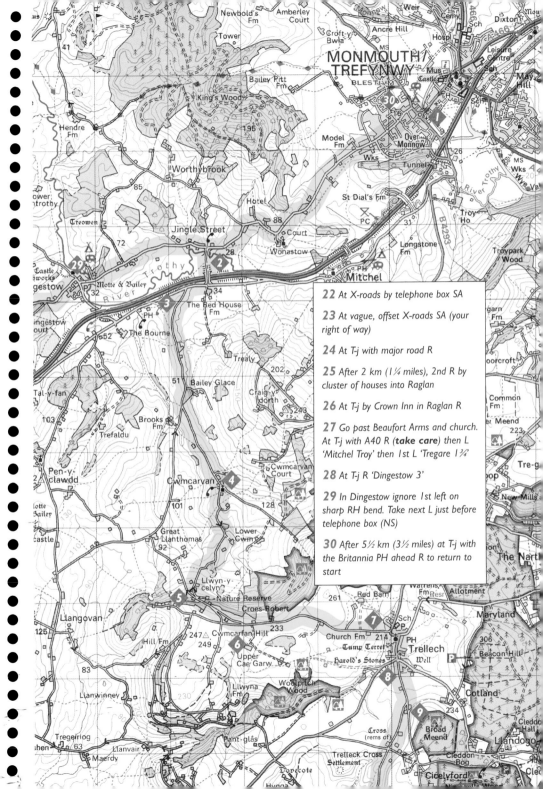

22 At X-roads by telephone box SA

23 At vague, offset X-roads SA (your right of way)

24 At T-j with major road R

25 After 2 km (1¼ miles), 2nd R by cluster of houses into Raglan

26 At T-j by Crown Inn in Raglan R

27 Go past Beaufort Arms and church. At T-j with A40 R (**take care**) then L 'Mitchel Troy' then 1st L 'Tregare 1¾'

28 At T-j R 'Dingestow 3'

29 In Dingestow ignore 1st left on sharp RH bend. Take next L just before telephone box (NS)

30 After 5½ km (3½ miles) at T-j with the Britannia PH ahead R to return to start

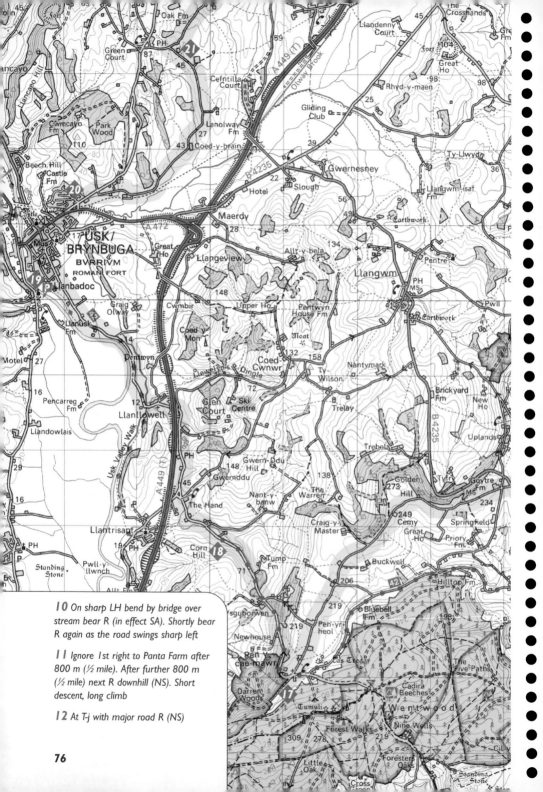

10 On sharp LH bend by bridge over stream bear R (in effect SA). Shortly bear R again as the road swings sharp left

11 Ignore 1st right to Panta Farm after 800 m (½ mile). After further 800 m (½ mile) next R downhill (NS). Short descent, long climb

12 At T-j with major road R (NS)

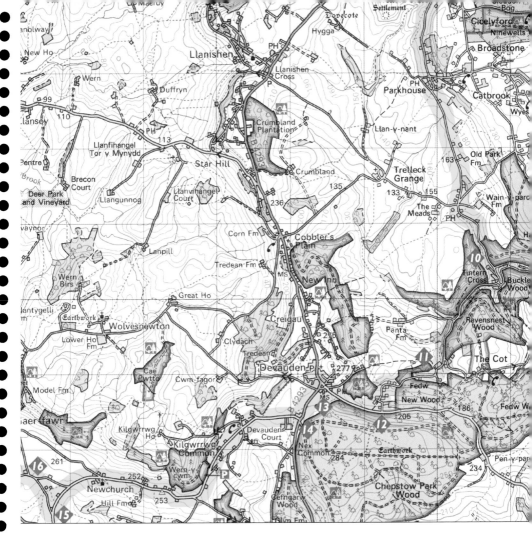

13 After 1 km (¾ mile) climb, opposite Masons Arms PH in Devauden bear L by large triangle of grass then L again at X-roads after 100 m (yd)

14 After 800 m (½ mile) 1st R by small triangle of grass 'Kilgwrrwg ½, Newchurch 2, Gaerllwyd 3'. Lovely ridge ride

15 1 km (¾ mile) after church in Newchurch R sharply back on yourself by small triangle of grass

'Gaer Fawr 1'. Climb hill

16 With small breeze block shed ahead bear L (in effect SA) (NS) then at X-roads (with B4235) SA (NS)

17 At T-j with new, stone-built, grey-roofed house ahead R downhill (NS)

18 Fast descent. Go past Greyhound PH, under the A449 and alongside the embankments of the River Usk

19 In Usk, follow the road round past the church. At T-j at the end of square with a clocktower R Newport 12, Monmouth 15, Chepstow 13' then bear 1st L after 300 m (yd) 'Gwehelog'

20 At Give Way sign continue SA then after 400 m (yd) 1st R (NS)

21 At T-j after 4 km (2½ miles) R downhill (NS)

◀ three pages

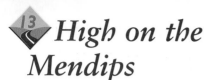# High on the Mendips

The Mendips are an outcrop of Carboniferous limestone stretching from Weston-super-Mare to Shepton Mallet, their most famous feature being the caves at Cheddar. The scenery is at times more reminiscent of the Yorkshire dales than southwest England, with squat grey stone houses and drystone walling.

The best views are to be found by making two detours from the main route, each of 400 m (½ mile), to the radio masts near Charterhouse and to the edge of the steep southern slopes west of Priddy.

The ride skirts the steep hills of the western end of the range and climbs via Winscombe and Shipham to its highest point 260 m (870 ft) near Tynings Farm. It continues along the top of the ridge to Chewton Mendip, then brings you back via the towering cliffs of Cheddar Gorge, the tourist complex of Cheddar and the quieter pleasures of Axbridge.

Start

The Square, Axbridge

P Long-term parking in Meadow Street, Axbridge

Distance and grade

59 km (37 miles)

Moderate/strenuous

Terrain

The Mendips are shaped like a whale's back. The ride climbs gently to the top and drops dramatically through the Cheddar Gorge

Nearest railway

Yatton, 10½ km (6½ miles) from Shipham

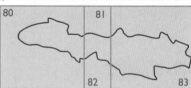

Axbridge · Winscombe · Star · Shipham · Charterhouse

King John's Hunting Lodge, Axbridge 2

An early 15th-century merchant's timber-framed house that has been extensively restored and converted into a museum of local history and archaeology. It has no apparent connection with King John, or with hunting, but was used as an ale house in the 17th and 18th centuries.

Lillypool Cider and Cheese Farm, Shipham 11

The farm dates back to the 18th century and houses an exhibition of farming equipment and cider mills. There is a café, children's play area and nature trail, and local cider, cheese, homemade pickles and chutneys are for sale.

Chewton Cheese Dairy, Priory Farm, Chewton Mendip 21

One of the few dairies left making traditional Cheddar cheese from Fresian and Ayrshire herds. Morning coffee, farmhouse lunches and cream teas.

Cheddar Showcaves 29

These spectacular caves within the limestone gorge are an attraction of outstanding natural beauty. There are magnificent crystalline formations that have taken over half a million years to form. The Cheddar Caves Museum displays various archeological finds.

Refreshments

Lamb PH🍴, plenty of choice in **Axbridge**
Waldegrave Arms PH🍴, **East Harptree**
Hunters Lodge Inn🍴, New Inn🍴,
Queen Victoria Inn🍴, **Priddy**
Tea shop at Cheese Farm, **Chewton Mendip**
Plenty of choice in **Cheddar**
Waldegrave Arms PH🍴, **East Harptree**

East Harptree

Litton

Chewton Mendip

Priddy

Cheddar

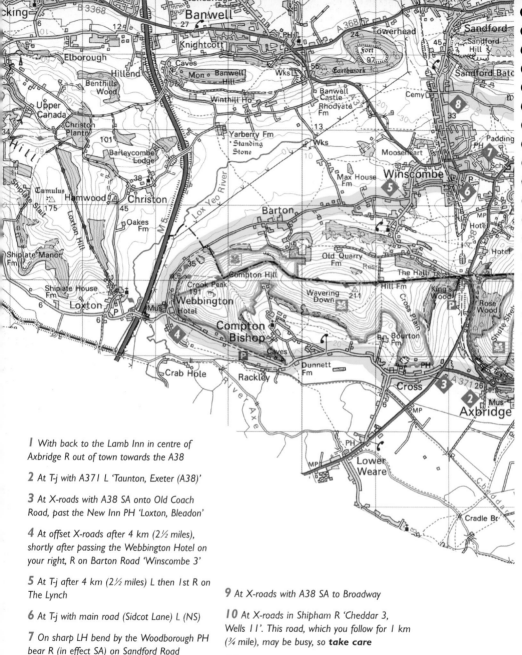

1 With back to the Lamb Inn in centre of Axbridge R out of town towards the A38

2 At T-j with A371 L 'Taunton, Exeter (A38)'

3 At X-roads with A38 SA onto Old Coach Road, past the New Inn PH 'Loxton, Bleadon'

4 At offset X-roads after 4 km (2½ miles), shortly after passing the Webbington Hotel on your right, R on Barton Road 'Winscombe 3'

5 At T-j after 4 km (2½ miles) L then 1st R on The Lynch

6 At T-j with main road (Sidcot Lane) L (NS)

7 On sharp LH bend by the Woodborough PH bear R (in effect SA) on Sandford Road

8 Almost 1½ km (1 mile) after the Woodborough PH, shortly after passing the glazing company on right and dental surgery on left, as road flattens, 1st R on Shipham Lane (NS)

9 At X-roads with A38 SA to Broadway

10 At X-roads in Shipham R 'Cheddar 3, Wells 11'. This road, which you follow for 1 km (¾ mile), may be busy, so **take care**

11 Shortly after the brow of the hill, just before Lillypool Cider Farm (good tea stop) L 'Charterhouse'

➡ **two pages**

29 *Through Cheddar Gorge and Cheddar. Opposite the Butchers Arms PH on your left R on Tweentown 'Weston-super-Mare' (A371)*

30 *After 800 m (½ mile), opposite the Catholic church, L on Lower North Street 'Baptist Church'*

31 *At T-j with A371, opposite shop, R then shortly L on Station Road, 'B3151 Wedmore'*

32 *2nd R, into Valley Line Industrial Estate, then on to Axbridge Cycleway*

33 *At end of cycleway, at T-j with main road L then L again 'Axbridge'*

12 Steady then steep climb to the plateau. After 5½ km (3½ miles), L at X-roads 'Burrington 3½, Blagdon 2¼ (After 400 m (yd), 1st L to radio masts for fine views or on to trig point for even better ones!). **For short cut** turn R at the X-roads 'Priddy 3½, Cheddar 5½ and follow signs for Cheddar back to the start

13 At T-j with B3134 R 'Cheddar 7½'

14 After 1½ km (1 mile), at truck repair yard L 'Compton Martin, West Harptree'

15 Go straight across two X-roads. **Take care** down steep hill!

16 At 3rd X-roads, with Mead Cottage ahead and a sign for 'Western Lane' near your right pedal (!), L

17 At the end of Middle Street, at T-j by the stores in East Harptree, R

18 After 1 km (¾ mile) at T-j beneath telephone wires R (NS)

19 On sharp RH bend L 'Litton 1¼, Chewton Mendip 1'

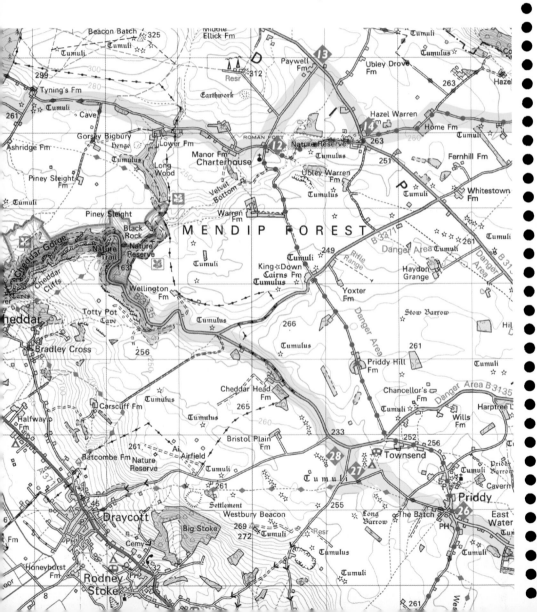

20 At T-j with B3114 R 'Chewton Mendip ½, Wells 6¼'

21 At X-roads with A39 SA then 1st R on Bray's Batch, bearing L at fork. You are now on Puppy Lane

22 At X-roads R (NS). At X-roads with A39 SA 'Cheddar 9¾, Burrington 9½ (1st R to Priory Farm for an excellent tea stop)

23 At T-j with B3135 R 'Priddy, Cheddar, Burrington'

24 At X-roads by Miners Arms PH L 'Priddy, Milton'

25 At X-roads by Hunters Lodge Inn R 'Priddy 1½, Cheddar 7'

26 In Priddy L at New Inn PH

27 After 1½ km (1 mile), at T-j R (NS) (detour L for 800 m (½ mile) for fine views to the south)

28 At T-j with B3135 L 'Cheddar 5'

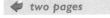 two pages

Start

The Square, Wilton

 P On side streets or on roads out of town

14 *A circle around Salisbury via Alderbury, Porton and the Woodfords*

Starting from the historic town of Wilton, the ride leaves the Nadder Valley and crosses the downland to the south to drop into the lovely Ebble Valley. It goes east through Odstock and Nunton and follows

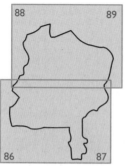

the valley of the River Avon to the first available bridge crossing at Downton, then back north to Alderbury. The route enters a military landscape, passing the research units at Porton Down and Boscombe Down, which may well send a shiver up your spine. On the other side of the A345, the route continues along the River Avon through the charming Woodford villages before a last downland climb to return to Wilton.

 Distance and grade

62 km (39 miles)

Easy/moderate

Terrain

Three climbs of 76 m (250 ft): one south from Wilton to cross the ridge, the second from Alderbury north-east towards Pitton and the third, the least lovable, coming at the end of the ride, between Lower Woodford and the A360

 Nearest railway

Salisbury, 3 km (2 miles)

 Refreshments

Silver Plough PH 🍺🍺, **Pitton**
Fox and Goose PH 🍺, **Coombe Bissett**
Yew Tree PH 🍺, **Odstock**

Wilton   Coombe Bissett   Nunton   Alderbury

Places of interest

Salisbury I

Salisbury, the county town of Wiltshire, lies at the heart of this route. It is situated at the confluence of the rivers Avon, Bourne, Nadder and Wylye and remains a thriving market town with many places of interest.

Salisbury Cathedral I

The cathedral was refounded in Salisbury in 1220 and took 38 years to complete, and the spire that towers to 120 m (404 ft) was added by the end of the century. It has a uniformity of style and there is an entrance for every month of the year, a window for every day and a column for every hour. Among the tombs within the cathedral is that of William Longespere who witnessed the signing of the Magna Carta of which one of the four remaining copies is kept in the library over the east walk.

Old Sarum

This lies to the north of the present city and was the site of the original cathedral and a castle. Friction between the Church and State in such close proximity led to the refoundation of the cathedral in its present location and the subsequent decline of Old Sarum.

▲ Salisbury Cathedral

Farley

Porton

Great Durnford

Middle Woodford

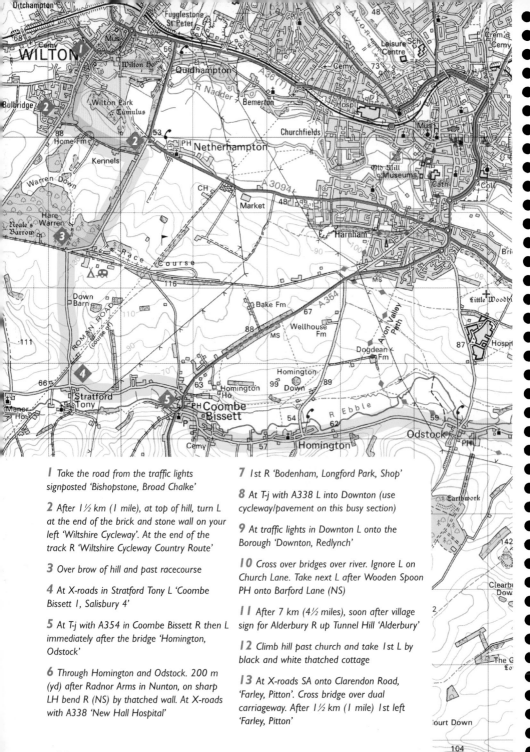

1 Take the road from the traffic lights signposted 'Bishopstone, Broad Chalke'

2 After 1½ km (1 mile), at top of hill, turn L at the end of the brick and stone wall on your left 'Wiltshire Cycleway'. At the end of the track R 'Wiltshire Cycleway Country Route'

3 Over brow of hill and past racecourse

4 At X-roads in Stratford Tony L 'Coombe Bissett 1, Salisbury 4'

5 At T-j with A354 in Coombe Bissett R then L immediately after the bridge 'Homington, Odstock'

6 Through Homington and Odstock. 200 m (yd) after Radnor Arms in Nunton, on sharp LH bend R (NS) by thatched wall. At X-roads with A338 'New Hall Hospital'

7 1st R 'Bodenham, Longford Park, Shop'

8 At T-j with A338 L into Downton (use cycleway/pavement on this busy section)

9 At traffic lights in Downton L onto the Borough 'Downton, Redlynch'

10 Cross over bridges over river. Ignore L on Church Lane. Take next L after Wooden Spoon PH onto Barford Lane (NS)

11 After 7 km (4½ miles), soon after village sign for Alderbury R up Tunnel Hill 'Alderbury'

12 Climb hill past church and take 1st L by black and white thatched cottage

13 At X-roads SA onto Clarendon Road, 'Farley, Pitton'. Cross bridge over dual carriageway. After 1½ km (1 mile) 1st left 'Farley, Pitton'

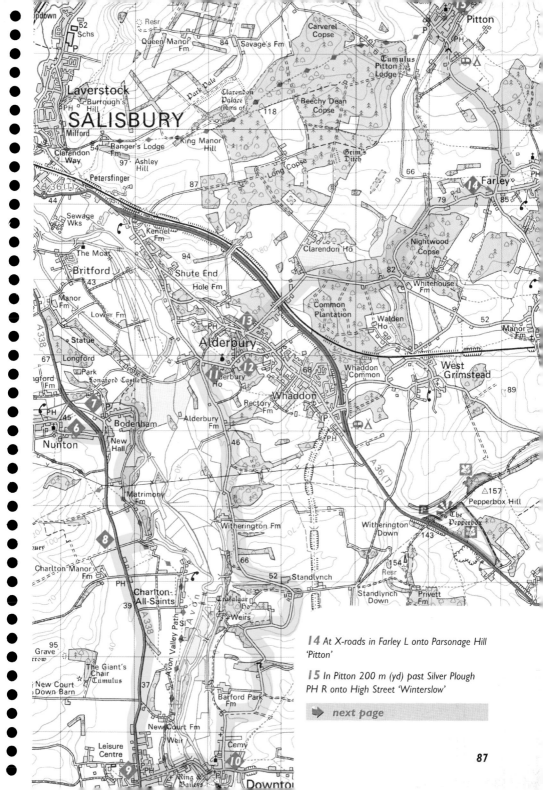

14 At X-roads in Farley L onto Parsonage Hill 'Pitton'

15 In Pitton 200 m (yd) past Silver Plough PH R onto High Street 'Winterslow'

➡️ *next page*

15 In Pitton 200 m (yd) past Silver Plough PH R onto High Street 'Winterslow'

16 At X-roads SA 'Andover, Stockbridge'

17 At X-roads with A30 SA through gates to cross Porton Down

18 Through Porton to X-roads with A338. SA 'Amesbury 5'

19 50 m (yd) before the busy A345 turn R onto track alongside perimeter fence by Crash Exit sign 'Byway to Amesbury'. The first 400 m (yd) are the toughest. At T-j with road L. At X-roads with A345 SA

20 Through Great Durnford, at T-j R 'Woodford, Wilton', then L at T-j by Bridge at Woodford PH 'Salisbury, Wilton'

21 For link to route west of Wilton, at telephone box in Middle Woodford R 'Great Wishford 3'

22 For return to Wilton, go through Middle Woodford and 1½ km (1 mile) after Lower Woodford R 'Wilton'

23 Steep climb to X-roads. SA 'Wilton 2'

24 At roundabout SA 'Town Centre'

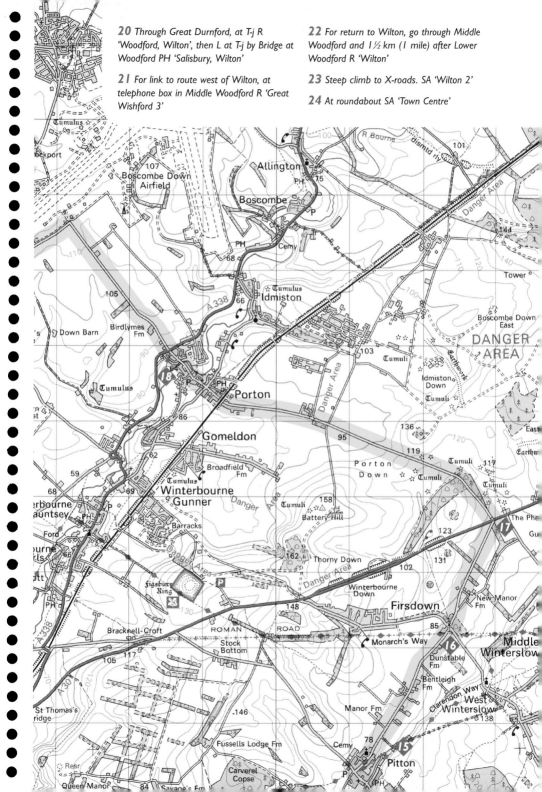

Steep Cotswold hills between Bristol and Bath

A short but demanding ride, this route gives you hard climbs and fast descents, panoramic views and a great dollop of mud near Lower Hamswell. The southern end of the Cotswolds near Bath has some of the steepest roads in the region and the off-road tracks are similar, with hillsides falling away very steeply either side of Lansdown Hill. The climbs are rewarded with fine views into the Avon Valley.

 Start

Upton Cheyney, just north of the A431 Bristol to Bath Road

P Near the Upton Inn in Upton Cheyney.

 Distance and grade

18 km (11 miles)

Moderate/strenuous

 Terrain

Lots of steep climbs and descents. Mud near Lower Hamswell

Nearest railway

Bath or Keynsham

 Refreshments

Upton PH, **Upton Cheyney**

Upton Cheyney

Brockham End

Off-road riding tips

- Padded shorts and gloves make off-road riding more comfortable

- If there is any possibility of rain, take something waterproof. Never underestimate the effects of wind-chill when you are wet, even in summer

- In wet and cold conditions, keep a layer of warm clothes next to the skin – thermal underwear or wool

- After fixing a puncture, check the inside of the tyre for embedded thorns before replacing the inner tube. A screwdriver is useful for winkling out difficult thorns

- Lower your saddle when going down steep off-road sections, keep the pedals level, stand up out of the saddle to let your legs absorb the bumps and keep your weight over the rear wheel

- Carry a water bottle in the bottle carrier and keep it filled, particularly on hot days

- Take a compass with you for crossing moorland or in poor visibility and know how to use it

- Good equipment doesn't make you a good cyclist. The only bad cyclists are those who show no consideration to others, whether by weaving around, failing to indicate or riding on pavements in on-road situations, or by failing to follow the countryside code, and showing no respect to walkers and horseriders when off-road

Langridge

Tadwick

Lower Hamswell

1 Go uphill from the Upton Inn for 400 m (yd)

2 As the road swings left, bear R (in effect SA) up Lansdown Lane

3 Climb steadily on tarmac, then track to the golf course

4 Keep wall and wood to your left and golf course to your right. Cross a major track at right angles (this is the drive to the golf club, a private road) and continue until reaching a junction of tracks at the end of the wood. Turn sharply L alongside the edge of the wood (maybe muddy)

5 At T-j with tarmac R. At T-j with the road R for 150 m (yd)

6 Just before reaching the second clump of trees, L through a wicket gate and across the field towards the gate in the stone wall

7 Before the signpost, bear R down the broad track. This soon becomes a fine descent

8 At T-j by barn at the bottom R. At T-j with road L. At next T-j L again

9 Climb for 1 km (¾ mile), ignore the 1st lane/No Through Road on the left to Tadwick Farm. Continue climbing steeply for 300 m (yd) and take the next L

10 After 200 m (yd), as the lane turns left more steeply downhill towards the farm, by a metal gate, turn R uphill on to track which follows hedgerow on the left. After 100 m (yd), bear L downhill. Maybe rutted and/or muddy

11 Cross the stream and climb on tarmac. At X-roads SA

12 At next X-roads SA 'Beach 1, Upton Cheyney 1½'

13 1st R 'Beach 1', then after 100 m (yd), bear R on the No Through Road. Tarmac becomes track. At the bottom, follow the stone stream bed to the L. You will probably have to push for a short stretch

14 Descend to cross the stream and follow the track as it climbs, levels out, then turns to tarmac at Coldharbour Farm. At T-j with road L then immediately L 'Upton Cheyney'

15 At X-roads SA 'Upton Cheyney' to return to start

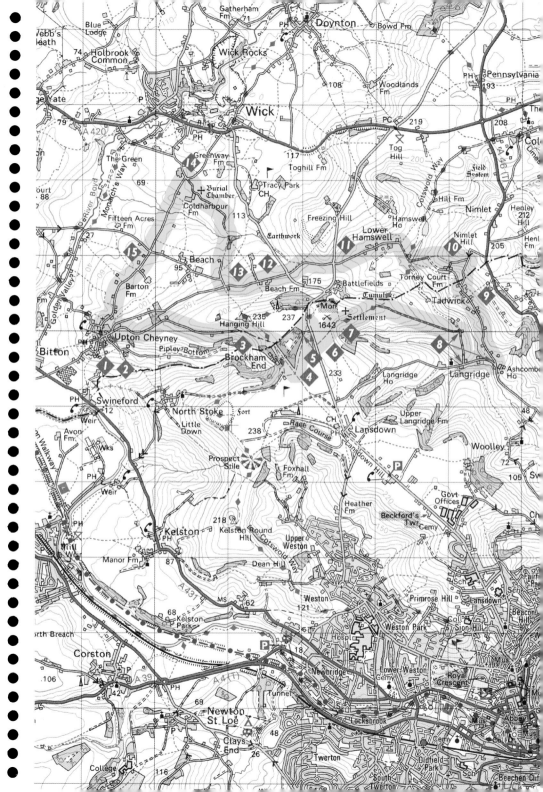

2 *Ancient earthworks around Avebury*

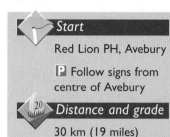

Start

Red Lion PH, Avebury

P Follow signs from centre of Avebury

Distance and grade

30 km (19 miles)

Moderate

*T*his ride would be easy but for the wild Wansdyke section, which is well worth doing for the sense of history and magnificent views although it may involve some pushing. It links the superb ridges of Cherhill Down and Wansdyke and even takes in a section of the most famous ancient road of all in this area: the first couple of miles of the Ridgeway.

▲ *Avebury village and stone circle*

Avebury

Knoll Down

Cherhill Down

Shepherd's Shore

Terrain

Chalk downland, ancient tracks, rough section on Wansdyke. Climb of 91 m (300 ft) on to Cherhill Down, otherwise mainly ridge riding.

Nearest railway

Pewsey, 8 km (5 miles) from the Wansdyke section lying to the south of East Kennett

Refreshments

Red Lion PH 🍺, tea shops, **Avebury**

Places of interest

Avebury I

The main part of the village lies within a Neolithic stone circle encompassing an area of about 28 acres. The outer stone circle once comprised up to 100 stones, some weighing as much as 100 tons. The site does not share the fame of its neighbour Stonehenge, but its importance was regarded by the antiquarian John Aubrey (1629–97) as great enough for him to persuade Charles II to visit, stating that it 'exceeded Stonehenge as a Cathedral exceeds a parish church'. The Alexander Keiller museum in the village tells much of the story of Avebury and other monuments nearby.

Silbury Hill

South of Avebury is Silbury Hill, the largest man-made mound in Europe.

West Kennet Long Barrow

This 5000-year-old site is one of the largest chambered tombs in Britain.

East Kennett

1 With your back to the PH, R down the No through road towards the church

2 100 m (yd) after the church on the right and just past the Old Vicarage to your left turn R onto tarmac lane. Road narrows to path. At fork by white railings bear R. At triangle of grass by Swan Cottage bear R (in effect SA)

3 Opposite barns on left turn R 'Ancient Monument'

4 Ignore gate on right to Windmill Hill. Go SA in same direction onto grassy track. Shortly after brow of hill enter copse and turn immediately L sharply back on yourself. At T-j with better stone-based track bear L (in effect SA)

5 At X-roads with main road (A4) SA onto track. After 400 m (yd) 1st track R along top of ridge (earthworks)

6 At T-j at end L uphill to barn and through gate on right. At top of hill, follow main track round to the R for the monument and fine views **or** carry SA onto grassy track for continuation of route

7 Follow in same direction with earthworks on the right. Descend through two bridlegates towards strip of pine trees

8 At start of pine trees turn R towards masts. Follow fence for 2½ km (1½ miles). Ignore two bridlegates to the left with tracks climbing steeply to the masts. Continue into and out of woodland on contouring track

9 At sign for Morgan's Hill Nature Reserve, sharply L back on yourself through bridlegate

10 Follow Wansdyke, the obvious earthworks, towards the main road (A361). At a copse, you will have to detour L then R to return to route. (This section may be very rough)

11 Cross road then L and R towards new house to get up onto Wan dyke. The going is very rough to begin with and you will have to push but it does improve

12 For the next 10 km (6 miles) the route follows Wansdyke. The earthworks themselves are impossible to lose; the best route, however, may be to the R, to the L or on top of the ridge, and comprehensive instructions would be meaningless. It is a beautiful section, so it does not matter if it is slow

13 The route descends to the Alton Barnes-Marlborough road, bearing away to the R of Wansdyke for the last few hundred yards

14 At T-j with road L then after ¾ mile 1st road L 'West Overton 2, East Kennett 1'

15 In East Kennett, just before 'School' sign R 'West Overton 1' then very shortly L alongside stone wall

16 At X-roads with main road (A4) SA on to Ridgeway. Ignore 1st byway to the left as you climb hill. After 2½ km (1½ miles) next L on broad track 'Byway' to return to Red Lion PH in Avebury

17 Cross main road (A4) on to Ridgeway and take 2nd L (byway) down into Avebury

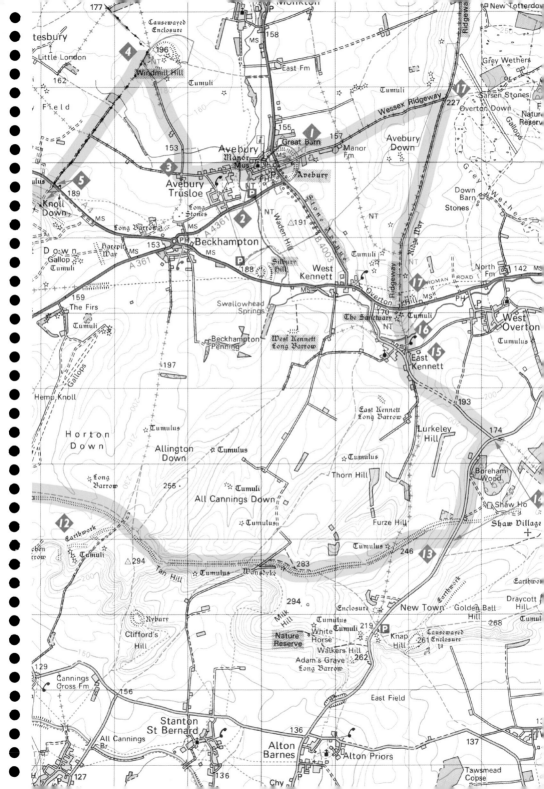

Over Dundry Hill and along little-known tracks southwest of Bristol

3

*T*his ride covers a wide variety of terrain very close to Bristol and climbs to the top of the ridge that forms Dundry Hill. There are two steep climbs and one muddy descent. The route provides good views across the Bristol Channel to Wales and back over Bristol.

Start

The Angel PH, Long Ashton, southwest of Bristol

P Along the Long Ashton road or in Ashton Court

Distance and grade

27 km (17 miles)
///// Moderate

Terrain

Two steep climbs – 140 m (450 ft) to the top of Barrow Hill, 150 m (500 ft) to the top of Dundry Hill.
Warning: *much of this ride, particularly the first off-road section on Barrow Hill and the descent from Dundry can be very muddy through the winter and after prolonged rain*

Nearest railway

Bristol Temple Meads

Refreshments

*The Angel PH ♥, **Long Ashton***
*The Bungalow Inn PH ♥, **Redhill** (just off the route, south of instruction 8)*
*Crown Inn PH ♥, **Regil** (just off the route, south of instruction 12)*
*Princes Motto PH ♥♥, **Barrow Gurney***

Long Ashton   Barrow Hill   Lulsgate Bottom   Kingdown

Off-road riding tips

- Keep some spare dry clothes and shoes in the car to change into and carry some bin liners in the car to put dirty, wet clothes in

- In very wet weather, keep other possessions dry by carrying them in two sets of plastic bags

- If your brake blocks, look as though they are wearing thin, take a spare set with you. New brake blocks are much cheaper than new rims

- Good energy foods that don't take up much space are dates, figs, dried fruit and nuts

- Always thank people who make way for you

- Always take a few coins for emergencies

- Always allow extra time when planning a trip for delays caused by punctures, getting lost and so on

- If you forget your lock, take your saddle and front wheel with you when you leave the bike. This is not recommended for any length of time and it is best to leave someone with the bikes if possible

- When riding in a group, plan the ride with the weakest person in mind. The fastest riders should go ahead and open gates for the rest of the group, shutting them afterwards, thus balancing out the difference in strength

Upper Littleton

Dundry Hill

Barrow Gurney

1 With back to The Angel PH L through Long Ashton

2 After 4 km (2½ miles), at T-J with B3130 L under bypass. Ignore R to Weston on A370, take next R up Barrow Court Lane (no through road). Follow road to end, ignoring Slade Lane to left

3 Where road ends, bear L towards conifer wood. Follow track uphill over X-roads of tracks ('Avon Cycleway Link'), keeping wood to your right (mud after rain) as far as gate

4 Through gate, SA for 30 m (yd) through grass. R on track, continue in same direction through middle of field, roughly parallel with pine trees to the right. Join better track and go through grey metal gate

5 Pass barn on your left, 100 m (yd) after road surface improves, L onto track. At T-j with tarmac R. At T-j with road L

6 At next T-j L. At A38 L then R 'Felton, Winford, Chew Magna'. After cattle grid 1st R, passing church on your left. Opposite church, fork R towards houses

8 Follow along edge of field on grassy surface to house with round oast house tower. Soon after surface improves near to oast tower, leave main track and fork L towards green pavilion. Keep to edge of field

9 At T-j of tracks R down broad track to road. At T-j with road L then 1st road R

10 At X-roads L past Five Gates 'Regil'. After about 1½ km (1 mile), sharply back on yourself by metal gate (this section may be overgrown)

11 Pass a quarry on your left. At T-j with road L to the brow of hill then R. **Not** Frog Lane but the stony track to the R of it

12 At X-roads by Crown Hill Farm, SA onto track. At T-j of tracks after 400 m (yd) near barn at bottom of hill turn R

13 At road L. At X-roads SA down Littleton Lane 'Upper Littleton ¼'

14 Ignore 1st R to Hazel End Farm after 800 m (½ mile). Shortly, take next R and climb steeply to top

15 At T-j with road L. Ignore 1st road to the right. After 200 m (yd) as road swings L downhill bear R (in effect SA) through white gate by house into field

16 Keep next to wall/hedge on the right to go down steep muddy track to bottom

17 Emerge at road, SA onto stony track. Past engineering firm, R at T-j, which takes you to road

18 At road SA onto track opposite. Emerge at A38, L on pavement then 1st R along Freeman's Lane, past farm, through gate to rejoin original route

19 Go to gate at edge of conifer wood and down track with wood to your left

20 At X-roads of tracks at corner of wood, leave outward route. R through gateway. Follow edge of field through three gates (blue bridleway arrows) to road

21 SA, through gate, over grassy track down through field to gate. Take lane to road. R on road past Princes Motto PH. 1st road L very steeply uphill. At T-j after 200 m (yd) bear L (in effect SA). At T-j after 2½ km (1½ miles) R on Weston Road to return to start

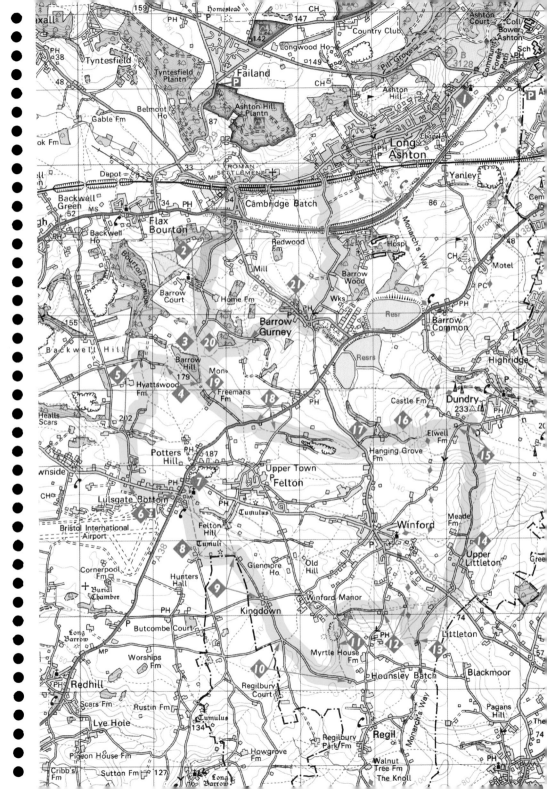

A slice of Cheddar and a taste of the Mendips

The Carboniferous limestone of the Mendips provides a marked contrast to the surrounding countryside. The ride climbs the Mendips twice, offering panoramic views across the Bristol Channel and over the Somerset Levels and moors. There are two steep descents, one narrow and stony through woodland, the other somewhat broader, through forestry plantation. The top ridge may be muddy. The area is also popular with walkers and horses, so show consideration, letting others pass and thanking them when they let you pass.

 Places of interest

Cheddar Gorge 1
The famous gorge is actually a collapsed cavern and runs for approximately 1½ km (1 mile) to the north-east of the village. The thickly wooded slopes and cliffs rise up to 460 m (1500 ft) above the roadway. Much of the area is owned by the National Trust. Roman coins and remains of prehistoric man have been found in the caves in the gorge, some of which are open to the public.

Burrington Combe 6
Another gorge, less spectacular than Cheddar. Augustus Toplady (1740–78) wrote the lines of the famous hymn 'Rock of ages cleft for me' while sheltering from a storm here.

 Start

The Edelweiss Restaurant, opposite the Cheddar Caves Information Booth at the lower end of Cheddar's main street

P The nearer the centre of Cheddar, the more expensive the car parks

 Distance and grade

29 km (18 miles)
Strenuous

 Terrain

Two steep climbs from north and south of the Mendips. Forest tracks, open moorland, farm tracks

 Nearest railway

Yatton, 10 km (6 miles) from the route at Rowberrow

Cheddar

King Down Farm

Beacon Batch

▲ Cheddar Gorge

Refreshments

Lots of choice in **Cheddar**
The Swan PH 🍺, **Rowberrow**
(just off the route between
instructions 7 and 8)

Read's Cavern

1 From the Edelweiss Restaurant, take the minor road out of Cheddar (to the left of St Andrews Road)

2 Pass Cheddar driving range on your left. At T-j L for 300 m (yd) as far as signpost for Hilltops B&B. L then R, leaving Bradley Cottage on your left

3 Follow this grassy track towards copse, following blue arrows and signs for Daycott. Continue uphill through gate with two large wooden posts. Climb steeply on narrow stony track, then more gently on broad farm track through several gates, eventually descending to the road

4 At X-roads with road (B3135) SA 'Compton Martin, Harptree'. After 1½ km (1 mile) 1st road L 'Charterhouse'. At X-roads near to Charterhouse church SA, then after 800 m (½ mile) 1st L on bridleway towards masts

5 Keep to left of mast. At trig point, continue in same direction towards top corner of plantation. At T-j of bridleways R then L to wood. There will be muddy stretches at all times of the year on the 3 km (2 miles) section between the masts and the start of the wood. These will be at their worst from winter to late spring. The two alternatives are: drop down on the road through Burrington Combe then cut southwest to rejoin the route beneath Dolebury Warren **or**, for a shorter ride, follow the road from the X-roads at Charterhouse to Tynings Farm and rejoin the route at instruction 10

6 Straight descent through wood to gap between poles. After 50 m (yd), at X-roads of tracks L on good stony track through woodland

7 After 1½ km (1 mile), in a small clearing with a green gate ahead and left of you turn L, passing a field, then stables on your right. (Keep a sharp eye out for this instruction)

8 Pass the pink, white and cream houses on your left, keeping to unmetalled track. At X-roads of bridleways SA, following blue arrow signs for Cheddar

9 Cross stream to your left and join forestry track coming up from the left. At X-roads of tracks SA to Tyning's Farm. Through farm to road

10 At road SA, with wall on your right. After 300 m (yd), as road bends R, SA 'Road unsuitable for motor vehicles'

11 Where this bears L into quarry SA down steep bridlepath into Cheddar. In open field, take the broad track to the L and follow main track as it bends round to T-j with road

12 R on road (Hannay Road) then 1st L (Kent Street) to return to start

5 *Chalk Ridges north of Mere*

*T*he ride is on the western edge of the chalklands that run from the Dorset coast to Swindon and beyond. The highest point of the ride is on White Sheet Hill 240 m (800 ft), from where there are superb views of Somerset. This is also the site of a Neolithic camp.

Off-road riding tips

- Alter your starting point to take account of the wind direction so that you are not cycling back into the wind when you are tired

- Discretion is the better part of valour – do not be persuaded to do something that you feel is way beyond your abilities

- If you come across a blocked right of way or one you feel is in a terrible state of repair, report it to the Rights of Way Department at the County Council. The most effective means is to write a letter giving grid references

Start

Car park on the lane running east from the Red Lion Inn on the B3092 road (Mere to Maiden Bràdley) towards White Sheet Hill

P As above

Distance and grade

24 km (15 miles)
🚴🚴🚴🚴 Moderate/ strenuous

Terrain

Mainly broad chalk tracks and farm tracks. May be muddy after rain and in winter

Nearest railway

Gillingham, 11 km (7 miles) South of White Sheet Hill

Kilmington

Norton Ferris

▲ Steep climb from Rodmead farm

Places of interest

Stourhead 3

One of the earliest English Palladian mansions, Stourhead House was built for Sir Henry Hoare by Colen Cambell and completed in 1725. It is most famous for its grounds, which take the form of an idealised Italian landscape and include a grotto, a Temple of Apollo and the Bristol Cross which was brought from Bristol in the 18th century. They were laid by Henry Hoare II and the architect Henry Flitcroft starting in 1744.

Refreshments

Red Lion PH 🍴 🍷, **Kilmington**

Kingston Deverill

Monkton Deverill

Charnage Down

White Sheet Downs

1 L out of the car park down the hill to the B3092

2 At X-roads with B3092 SA onto track. The first 400 m (¼ mile) is a bit rough. To avoid the worst of the mud and roughest of the tracks, turn R on the road for 1½ km (1 mile) and rejoin the route at instruction 7. Turn R off the B3092 at a triangle of grass with a Norton Ferris sign down a No Through Road

3 At X-roads at the end of Kilmington Common by red-brick house R then after 400 m (¼ mile) at 2nd X-roads R again 'Kilmington'

4 At T-j by memorial stone L, then after 400 m (¼ mile), by a bench beneath a copper beech tree, R onto track

5 Gently downhill. Ignore field gates to the left. After 800 m (½ mile) L on track (no gate) 'Byway'

6 Rough section. Ignore gateways to the right. After 800 m (½ mile), with better track ahead, 1st R onto track towards distinctive round hill

7 Gently downhill to road. R then L down No through road

8 200 m (yd) past Elm Farm, on sharp RH bend, leave tarmac to go SA through gateway into field onto rough track running along LH field edge

9 Through gate into next field, through field and onto road

10 At road R towards Rodmead Farm and through farmyard. Through metal gate and bear L up steep chalk track with fine views opening up

11 *Follow directions carefully!* As track levels, at junction of tracks near gate (blue arrows and 2-way 'Bridleway' signs) L through gate heading across open field to another gate slightly left of straight ahead (11 o'clock). Go through the 2nd gate and L gently downhill alongside fence for 300 m (yd) until reaching a wicket gate with a blue bridleway sign. Turn R to contour along hillside towards the LH end of the wood

12 Go through gate near end of wood and contour along hillside towards the fence on your right. Follow this to the end, then bear down and across the field towards a bridlegate

13 Cross concrete track and through 2nd bridlegate then diagonally L across field to gate

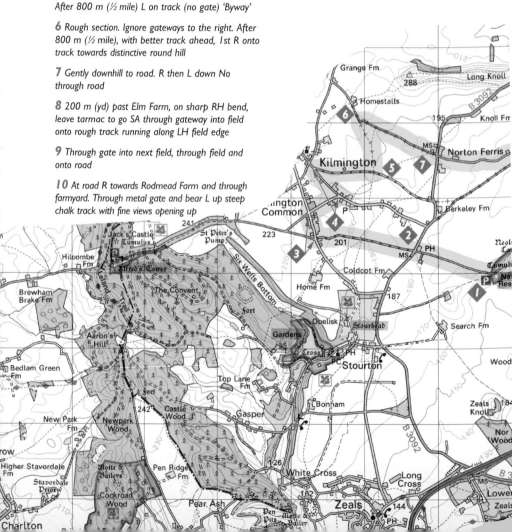

14 At T-j with road by signs for Gliding Club and near a telegraph pole with lines from all directions, turn R through village

15 At T-j (with B3095) by the church bear L (in effect SA)

16 On reaching sign for Monkton Deverill 1st R '7.5 ton weight limit', then 1st R again by metal gate, up a tarmac lane

17 At metal gate SA into field, taking the lower track next to the hedge

18 Through two more gates, closely spaced, then **ignore** obvious track that climbs steeply to right and carry along grassy valley bottom, passing a hawthorn tree on your left, heading towards gate

19 Through gate and climb out of valley on obvious track to another gate

20 On track through middle of field to yet another gate, then along RH edge of field to T-j with major track, with the A303 in sight and earshot

21 Turn R and follow this track for about 6½ km (4 miles), crossing the B3095 to White Sheet Hill. Follow main track back down to starting point and car park

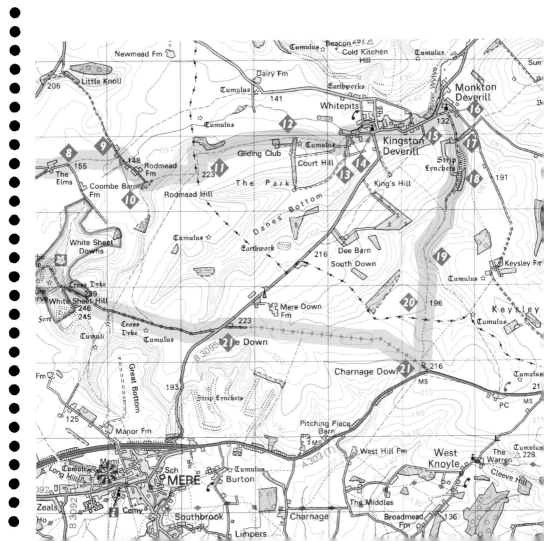

Ancient roads in Wiltshire

*T*he route of this ridge ride through Wiltshire downland follows the old Salisbury to Exeter coach road outwards and returns on the Roman road that used to run from the Mendips to Old Sarum via Grovely Wood. There are fine views of rolling Wiltshire countryside at several points. The route is entirely off-road although some of the surfaces are as good as roads, particularly on the return half, which is, consequently, much easier than the outward half.

◀ *Wilton House*

Wilton

Crouch's Down

Stockton Earthworks

Off-road riding tips

- If some vegetation gets stuck in your derailleur, remove it straightaway before it does any damage

- Anticipate hills by changing into the right gear before it gets tough

- Drink before you get thirsty and eat before you get hungry. Regular small amounts are better than a big lunch

- Leave no litter

- Make sure there is nothing loose and dangling (laces, daypack straps, pannier straps), which may get caught in the spokes, chain or pedals

- If there is any chance of cycling in twilight or darkness, take lights with you. As a precaution in winter, take a reflective belt and/or reflective strips for ankles and wrists – being visible is what matters most

- If carrying bikes on a car, stop regularly to check they are securely fixed

Great Ridge

Stockton Earthworks

Grovely Wood

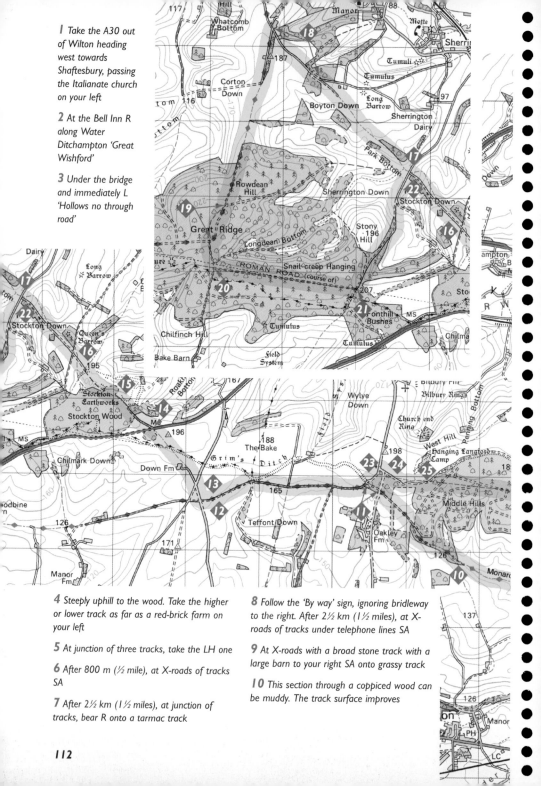

1 Take the A30 out of Wilton heading west towards Shaftesbury, passing the Italianate church on your left

2 At the Bell Inn R along Water Ditchampton 'Great Wishford'

3 Under the bridge and immediately L 'Hollows no through road'

4 Steeply uphill to the wood. Take the higher or lower track as far as a red-brick farm on your left

5 At junction of three tracks, take the LH one

6 After 800 m (½ mile), at X-roads of tracks SA

7 After 2½ km (1½ miles), at junction of tracks, bear R onto a tarmac track

8 Follow the 'By way' sign, ignoring bridleway to the right. After 2½ km (1½ miles), at X-roads of tracks under telephone lines SA

9 At X-roads with a broad stone track with a large barn to your right SA onto grassy track

10 This section through a coppiced wood can be muddy. The track surface improves

11 At the Wylye-Dinton road SA. Shortly after, at concrete track L 'Byway'

12 (For the next 5½ km (3½ miles), as far as Queens Barrow X-roads, this section forms part of both the outward and return route) Follow the concrete track for 2½ km (1½ miles)

13 At X-roads with tarmac road R. After 100 m (yd), at X-roads SA towards the pink house 'No MOD vehicles'

14 Through gate and wood to emerge at the busy A303 SA onto muddy track.

15 Emerge from woodland, carry on across grassland, bearing R (northwest), with Stockton earthworks to the right

16 At X-roads of tracks (Queens Barrow) SA through wide metal gate, keeping the wood on the right. Descend to road. (*Return trip rejoins route at this point)

17 At road L then R uphill on track

18 At metalled track L. Just before a collection of barns on the right turn L onto track between fence and trees

19 Once into a conifer forest with trees on both sides, ignore 1st left turn on stone track. After 1 km (¾ mile), shortly after sharp RH bend, next stone track L

20 Take 2nd L along well-made gravel track

21 After 2 km (1¼ miles), at T-j L steeply downhill. The surface improves and soon you rejoin the outward route (*)

22 Turn R uphill through gate. The byway bears L then rejoins the concrete track a little higher. Retrace your tracks from the outward leg for 5½ km (3½ miles) passing Queen's Barrow, Stockton earthworks and crossing the A303 (**take care**). At X-roads with road SA 'Teffont' then 1st L 'Byway' to rejoin the concrete track that leads to the Wylye–Dinton road

23 Do **not** turn R off this but follow it to the end as it turns to rough gravel to join the Wylye–Dinton road slightly north of the outward crossing

24 At road R, then L (in effect SA) on a sharp RH bend after 60 m (yd)

25 At the Simplex barn bear R

26 After passing a farm on the right, take the 2nd R by a triangle of grass where the telephone lines cross from left to right to follow the ridge through magnificent beech trees, past the red-brick farm back into Wilton

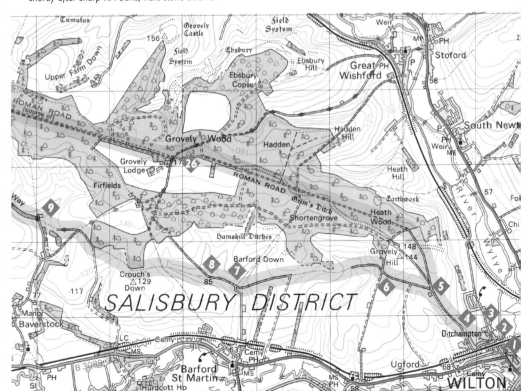

7 Ridge tracks and Ox Droves west of Wilton

Spread out fan-like to the west of Wilton are a series of valleys and ridges that provide some very enjoyable on-road and off-road cycling. The on-road rides tend to follow the valleys and the off-road, the ridges. This ride crosses the River Nadder to the south of Wilton and climbs past Hunt's Down through woodland to the main east-west ridge. A superb, easy track heads west between hedgerows, with views alternating to the north and south. The route drops to Alvediston, then climbs steeply to the parallel ridge to the south, the Ox Drove, which is a rougher track than the earlier ridge. A gentle 76 m (250 ft) descent to Broad Chalke via Church Bottom leaves you with one final climb past Flamstone Farm back to the first ridge and an exhilarating descent back to Wilton.

Start

The Square, Wilton

P On various side roads off the main roads out of town

Distance and grade

40 km (25 miles)

AAA Moderate

Terrain

Excellent off-road riding on the ridge between Hunt's Down, west– southwest to Middle Down, a steep descent and climb via Alvediston to reach the Ox Drove ridge further south, which is rougher and may be muddy. A final steep climb on sealed surface past Flamstone Farm to regain first ridge

Nearest railway

Salisbury, 5 km (3 miles) east of Wilton

Refreshments

Crown Inn PH 🍴🍷, **Alvediston**
Horseshoe PH 🍴🍷, **Ebbesbourne Wake** *1½ km ((1 mile) east of the route at Alvediston)*
Queens Head PH 🍷, **Broad Chalke**
White Hart PH 🍷, **Bishopstone**

Wilton   Hunt's Down   Fovant Hill   Middle Down   Alvediston

Off-road riding tips

- Do not expect your friendly bike shop to repair your bike at a moment's notice, particularly on a Friday in summer!

- Clean your bike of mud before expecting a mechanic to work on it

- When coming up behind a horse, give the rider plenty of warning with a big 'Hallooo'

- Leave a reasonable distance between you and the rider in front: you never know what obstacles he/she may come across

- Let someone know where you are going, particularly if it is winter and you are going to a remote area.

- The same off-road route can take much longer after rain or in the winter when tracks are softer, so plan accordingly

- If using British Rail, always phone in advance to check what the regulations are for the service you wish to use and if a reservation is required

- Plan a ride with the weakest person in mind

- To get an early start, prepare your equipment and bike the night before

- Make yourself a checklist that you can use whenever you go off on a ride, amending it for weekends away or for winter riding

- Aside from the whole bike, the most likely things to be stolen are: bicycle computer, panniers, lights, pump, saddle. If you can't be bothered to take the whole lot, at least take your wallet/purse and keys

Cow Down Hill   Ox Drove Ridge   Broad Chalke   Stoke Farthing   Flamstone Farm

1 From the traffic lights in the square in Wilton, take South Street 'Bishopstone 4, Broad Chalke 6'

2 1st R after the bridge 'Burcombe'

3 Pass a housing estate on left, take track L opposite house on the right and 'No entry' sign. The track is signposted 'Public right of way'

4 Steady climb to T-j at start of wood. Turn R by line of beech trees. Remember this point for return trip

5 Carry on climbing through woodland ignoring turnings until emerging onto ridge at edge of wood at major X-roads of tracks by a triangle of grass. Turn R. Remember this point for return trip

6 At T-j with more major track after 3 km (2 miles) bear L, then shortly, as main track swings left bear R (in effect SA) onto grassy track. At X-roads with tarmac after 5 km (3 miles) SA

7 After a further 4 km (2½ miles), at 2nd tarmac road, L to descend to Alvediston

8 At X-roads in Alvediston R 'Berwick St John, Shaftesbury' then 1st L up tarmac lane/track

9 130 m (430 feet) climb, steep at the end. At X-roads of tracks on the ridge with a barn ahead turn L

10 Follow the ridge on track, then on tarmac for 1½ km (1 mile) 'Handley'

11 At T-j SA onto track 'Byway to drove road'

12 At next road SA onto track 'Byway'

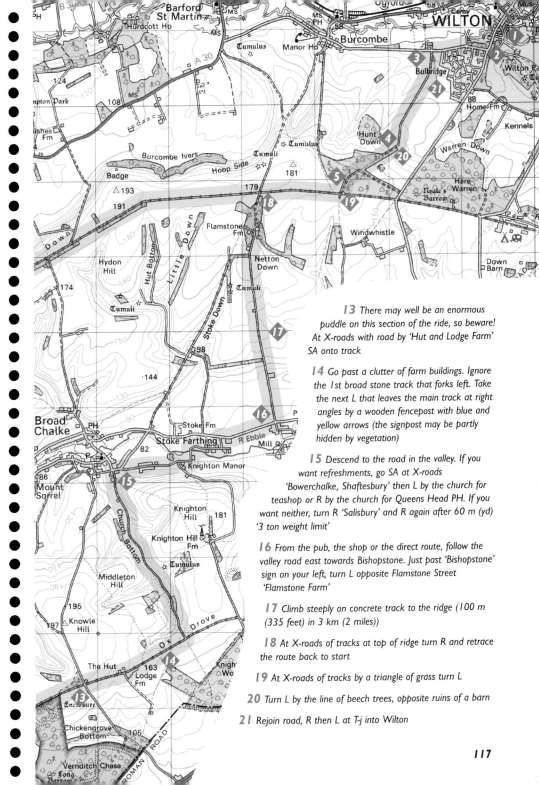

13 There may well be an enormous puddle on this section of the ride, so beware! At X-roads with road by 'Hut and Lodge Farm' SA onto track

14 Go past a clutter of farm buildings. Ignore the 1st broad stone track that forks left. Take the next L that leaves the main track at right angles by a wooden fencepost with blue and yellow arrows (the signpost may be partly hidden by vegetation)

15 Descend to the road in the valley. If you want refreshments, go SA at X-roads 'Bowerchalke, Shaftesbury' then L by the church for teashop or R by the church for Queens Head PH. If you want neither, turn R 'Salisbury' and R again after 60 m (yd) '3 ton weight limit'

16 From the pub, the shop or the direct route, follow the valley road east towards Bishopstone. Just past 'Bishopstone' sign on your left, turn L opposite Flamstone Street 'Flamstone Farm'

17 Climb steeply on concrete track to the ridge (100 m (335 feet) in 3 km (2 miles))

18 At X-roads of tracks at top of ridge turn R and retrace the route back to start

19 At X-roads of tracks by a triangle of grass turn L

20 Turn L by the line of beech trees, opposite ruins of a barn

21 Rejoin road, R then L at T-j into Wilton

117

West from Lambourn to the Ridgeway near Ogbourne St George

8

The route climbs out of Lambourn to cross the M4 close to Baydon. A fast tarmac descent down Marridge Hill drops you near Aldbourne, where two pubs may tempt you to stop for refreshments. A stiff climb out of Aldbourne takes you to the top of Ewin's Hill and through to the Ridgeway. The scenery is open and the views panoramic. You have a choice of continuing along the Ridgeway or taking the more direct course for Lambourn: going up Sugar Hill, along a few hundred yards of the Ermin Way, over Fognam Down and across some open gallops. Fine tracks drop you back at Farncombe Farm for a gentle roll back to Lambourn.

Start

The Red Lion PH in the centre of Lambourn

P On High Street (B4000) south out of Lambourn towards Hungerford

Distance and grade

36 km (22½ miles)
Moderate

Terrain

Good downland tracks. Three main climbs: 85 m (280 ft) from Lambourn to above Marridge Hill, 88 m (290 ft) from Aldbourne to Stock Lane and 91 m (300 ft) from Whiteshard Bottom to Whitefield Hill. Short, steep climb up Sugar Hill between B4192 and M4

Nearest railway

Hungerford, 11 km (7 miles) south of Lambourn

Refreshments

Lots of choice in **Lambourn**
Crown PH 🍺, Blue Boar PH 🍺, **Aldbourne**
Old Crown PH 🍺, just off the route in
Ogbourne St George

Lambourn — Coppington Down — Marridge Hill — Aldbourne — Southward Down — Ewin's Hill — Whiteshard Bottom

The Ridgeway over the North Wessex Downs

Geology
The Ridgeway over the Wessex Downs runs along the chalk formed in the Cretaceous period 120 million years ago. Along with chalk deposits, flint was laid down in horizontal beds and was used in prehistoric times for weapons and agricultural implements.

Flora and fauna
Chalk grassland that has been grazed by sheep but not improved with fertilizer provides a rich variety of flowers. The banks and ditches of the hillforts, especially Barbury Castle and Uffington Castle, provide an excellent opportunity to study the flora associated with chalk downland. The woodlands of the downs are sparse, mainly beech clumps or shelterbelts. The bird-life of the downs varies according to the seasons; swallows and swifts arrive in spring, while the berry-seeking fieldfares and redwings follow in autumn. The kestrel is the commonest bird of prey but occasional buzzards and sparrowhawks can be seen. Fallow, Sika and Roe deer can be seen in the woodland, especially in the evening. Fox and hare frequent fields and gallops.

Early Man
The Neolithic Long Barrows of Lambourn date from between 3400 BC and 2800 BC. The Long Barrows contained communal burial chambers that were first constructed of timber and later of sarsen stone. The Bronze Age Beaker Folk, who buried their dead with a drinking vessel, brought with them copper and later bronze tools and weapons. The Lambourn Seven Barrows are perhaps the finest examples of their round burial mounds. The hillfort is an Iron Age phenomenon (700 BC to 43 AD). Just below the Ridgeway runs Grim's Ditch; this linear territorial ditch is probably Iron Age in date and is thought to have demarcated the pastoral area of the West Berkshire Downs from the arable Vale of White Horse.

Horse racing
The gallops that abut the Ridgeway have developed since the late 18th century, when horse racing stables were first established on the Downs; the turf is springy and ideal for training purposes. Lambourn is the main racehorse centre although many downland villages have racing stables.

The Ridgeway Long-Distance Route
This Long-Distance Route was designated by the Countryside Commission in 1972 and opened the following year. It runs for 136 km (85 miles) from Avebury in Wiltshire to Ivinghoe Beacon in Buckinghamshire.

Round Hill Downs — Whitefield Hill — Shipley Bottom — Sugar Hill — Peaks Downs — Fognam Down — Row Down

1 With back to the Red Lion PH SA onto Parsonage Lane, left of church. After 300 m (yd) 1st L onto Baydon Road 'Baydon 3, Newbury 12¾'

2 Steady climb. After 2 km (1¼ miles), at X- roads of by-ways, by green barn to the left and grain silos to the right L 'By-way'

3 After 300 m (yd), at T-j by gate R onto gravel track 'Public Bridleway'

4 Where broad track turns left into field with gallops SA on narrower gravel track. At T-j with tarmac, by a metal barn R

5 At T-j with wider road (white line down middle) R. After 1½ km (1 mile) cross motorway bridge, then immediately L onto track parallel with M4

6 This track soon bears R away from M4. Follow it as it becomes a better stone-based track. Tracks merge from right then left. Surface turns to tarmac near farm

18 Steep climb. At corner of field by wood, as main track swings right (by-way to Aldbourne) bear L (in effect SA) along edge of wood

19 At road L. At T-j R 'Baydon 2, Newbury 17'

20 1st L over motorway 'Russley Park' and follow road to the right

21 On a sharp RH bend, after passing black and white timbered houses bear L (in effect SA) through gate 'By- way. Upper Lambourn 2½'

22 Follow this grassy track in the same direction through several gates and fields. At X-roads of by-ways, where the grassy track you have been following joins better stone track R between wire fence and hedgerow

23 Follow this track as it bears L uphill. At one point you will have to cross an open field with gallop markers. Watch out for charging horses! Join good, broad, stone track near green shed and bear L

24 At two X-roads of by-ways SA. At T-j with road L to return to start along outward route

12 At X-roads with road, at Stock Close Farm R. After 400 m (¼ mile), on sharp RH bend with chevrons L onto tarmac lane 'By-way to Whiteshard Bottom'

13 Fine steady descent. At fork (with tarmac lane leading uphill to left) bear R onto track 'By-way to Ridgeway'

14 At X-roads of tracks R 'Ridgeway. By-way'

15 At T-j with tarmac L 'Ridgeway. By-way', then at X-roads with road SA onto track 'Ridgeway. By-way'

16 At fork of tracks where Ridgeway divides bear R 'Ridgeway route for vehicles'

17 At X-roads with B4192 SA through gate 'By-way to Peaks Down'

7 At T-j by triangle of grass R

8 At T-j with B4192 R 'Cirencester'

9 In Aldbourne, by newly built houses 1st L onto Farm Lane

10 This becomes Southward Lane and climbs steadily. At fork R 'By-way to Ewin's Hill'

11 After 1½ km (1 mile) go past farm buildings. 800 m (½ mile) further 1st R onto track

A double loop in the southern Cotswolds near Hawkesbury Upton

A ride on the Cotswold escarpment along valleys and through woodland, passing many lovely Cotswold stone buildings. The ride starts at the high point with fabulous views out across the Vale of Severn. Over tracks and along field edges, the ride crosses the A46 after Bodkin Hazel Wood. Soon you have the unusual experience of crossing a landing strip – watch out for planes! The second loop descends through woodland, which is muddy after rain and in winter, down to Lower Kilcott before climbing again to Alderley. A final climb past Splatt's Barn will return you to the start.

Places of interest

Horton Court 3
A National Trust Cotswold manor house with a 12th-century Norman hall and Renaissance features. There is also a late Perpendicular ambulatory detached from the house.

Start

Somerset Monument, near Hawkesbury Upton, 40 km (25 miles) northeast of Bristol

P Some parking near the monument itself, or near the pond in Hawkesbury Upton

Distance and grade

27 km (17 miles)
Moderate

Terrain

The southern loop is fairly flat, the northern loop climbs 122 m (400 feet) from the low point in Lower Kilcott back up to the monument

Nearest railway

Yate (not open Sundays), 8 km (5 miles) from Horton; Stroud and Chippenham, both 18 km (11 miles) from Hawkesbury Upton

Highfield Farm

Widdenhill Farm

Off-road riding tips

- If using a jet spray to clean your bike, do not aim the hose directly at the houbs or bottom bracket – clean these parts from above

- Lubricate your bike after washing it or after a very wet ride, paying particular attention to the chain

- Experiment with saddle height, forwards and backwards adjustment of saddle, tilt of saddle up or down and height of the handlebars (do not exceed maximum height) until you find your most comfortable riding position

- The same off-road route can take much longer after rain or in the winter when tracks are softer, so plan accordingly

- Good energy foods that do not take up much space are dates, figs, dried fruit and nuts

- If you come across a blocked right of way or one you feel is in a terrible state of repair, report it to the Rights of Way Department at the County Council. The most effective means is to write a letter giving grid references

Somerset Monument

Lower Kilcott

Alderley

Hillesley

1st Loop

1 With back to the mounment L for 600 m (yd). At the village pond R 'Cotswold Way'

2 After 100 m (yd) L 'Horton 3.5 kilometres'. Follow track for 1½ km (1 mile) (mud after rain) to road

3 At road R. Follow for 1½ km (1 mile). At RH bend sharply L on broad track

4 Emerge at A46. **With great care**, R then L into wood, then immediately R

5. After 200 m (yd), at X-roads of tracks L through wooden gate to follow hedgerow

6 Follow main track across concrete farm track into next field. After 2nd stone wall L on to road

7 At road R for 800 m (½ mile). 10 m (yd) before the lodge on your right turn R onto stone-based track through gate by cypress hedge. Follow track as it turns R towards grey corrugated iron shed

8 Between buildings across landing strip and down into hollow. As track starts climbing, turn L along faint hedgerow opposite 3rd gate opening in stone wall on your right towards trees on horizon

9 At edge of the woodland R then L At X-roads with major track in the strip of woodland SA onto narrow track

10 Follow this track round to the R and exit woodland via wooden gate into the field

11 You are aiming directly for the A46 along the LH edge of the stone wall. The farmer is obliged to re-establish the track after ploughing. If he has not, please contact Gloucestershire Rights of Way Dept. At edge of wood by the road, follow the field round to the L for 10 m (yd) looking out for opening through the trees on your right. Cross A46 (**take care**) onto road opposite

12 1st R up single track lane 'Hawkesbury Upton 2½. At T-j L past Fox PH to start point

2nd Loop

13 From monument 300 m (yd) downhill on main road. As road bears L at junction of bridleways 1st R 'Lower kilcott 2 kilometres, Alderley 4 kilometres'

14 Through gate following blue arrow on well-defined track across field to wood

15 Through gate, take LH track, blue arrow. At times very muddy

16. Through metal gate at edge of wood. Follow blue arrow/white dot round edge of field. At T-j with track turn L through wooden gate

17 Fast descent to road. Turn L. After 1 km (¾ mile) just before road starts to climb, R on track over bridge 'Cotswold Way'

18 After 100 m (yd) at junction of bridleways L through gate with blue arrow and white dot

19 Follow track uphill through several gates to road. At road L downhill. Go through Hillesley, ignoring roads to right and left

20 Start to climb. As road bends L, opposite long metal gate on your right turn L up track

21 Through woodland, past Splatt Barn to rejoin outgoing route. L on road to monument

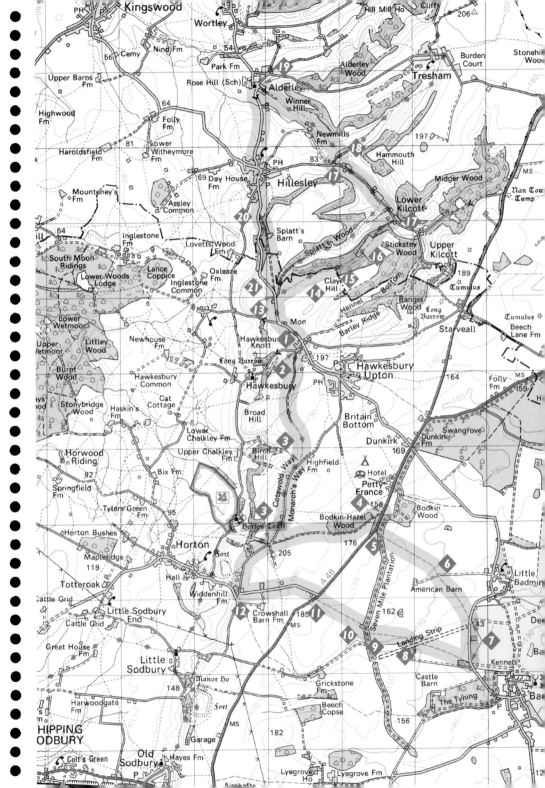

Notes

Notes

Useful addresses

British Cycling Federation

National Cycling Centre
Stuart Street
Manchester M11 4DQ
0870 871 2000
www.bcf.uk.com

The BCF co-ordinates and promotes an array of cycle sports and cycling in general. They are a good first point of contact if you want to find out more about how to get involved in cycling. The website provides information on upcoming cycle events and competitions.

CTC (Cyclists Touring Club)

Cotterell House
69 Meadrow
Godalming
Surrey GU7 3HS
01483 417217
www.ctc.org.uk

Britain's largest cycling organisation, promoting recreational and utility cycling. The CTC provides touring and technical advice, legal aid and insurance, and campaigns to improve facilities and opportunities for all cyclists. The website provides details of campaigns and routes and has an online application form.

The London Cycling Campaign

Unit 228
30 Great Guildford Street
London SE1 0HS
020 7928 7220
www.lcc.org.uk

The LCC promotes cycling in London by providing services for cyclists and by campaigning for more facilities for cyclists. Membership of the LCC provides the following benefits: London Cyclist magazine, insurance, legal advice, workshops, organised rides, discounts in bike shops and much more. You can join the LCC on its website.

Sustrans

Head Office
Crown House
37-41 Prince Street
Bristol BS1 4PS
General information line: 0117 929 0888
www.sustrans.org.uk

A registered charity, Sustrans designs and builds systems for sustainable transport. It is best known for its transformation of old railway lines into safe, traffic-free routes for cyclists and pedestrians and wheelchair users. Sustrans is developing the 13,000 km (8000 mile) National Cycle Network on traffic-calmed minor roads and traffic-free paths, to be completed by the year 2005 with major funding from the Millennium Commission.

Veteran Cycle Club

Membership Secretary
31 Yorke Road
Croxley Green
Rickmansworth
Herts WD3 3DW
www.v-cc.org.uk

A very active club, the VCC is concerned with the history and restoration of veteran cycles. Members enjoy organised rides and receive excellent publications relating to cycle history and club news.